You've had a stroke

The essential recovery handbook

If you've woken up confused, lying, half paralysed, in a hospital bed, and told that you've survived a stroke, then this is the book for you.

It's full of practical advice, from how to change your outlook on life to survive the psychological issues that you will encounter, through to dealing with all the financial and personal issues that your new life will throw at you.

Do not expect a medical dictionary, I am writing this from personal experience.

Do not expect a light read, you have to deal with a lot of pain to recover! But remember, it does get better.

I think I'll start with my own experience of stroke, well what I remember of it. Since, as part of my recovery I have trained myself not to dwell on the negative, my memories of my stroke are fleeting.

I vaguely remember the confusion, the panicked telephone call, the ambulance journey and the time spent in A & E. Other than that I have no real memory of how I ended up in a bed in a small room, on a hospital ward.

I woke up feeling groggy, and sure that something major was wrong. I have since found out that I had contracted encephalitis over a week before, and been on mind bending drugs for most of the time since then.

I had been allowed home, but one day later I was back.

"You've had a stroke" is the first thing I heard, and then I heard myself making funny noises trying to speak for the first time, not realising half of my mouth couldn't move.

I Instinctively tried to move all my limbs and…………..nothing, and then I descended into depression as I realised for the first time that half of my body no longer worked. The nurse left the room to leave me dealing with the bombshell that had just been dumped on me.

"What about work?"

"Will I need a wheelchair?"

"How will I drive?"

"Can I still have sex?"

The questions kept coming, but the answers evaded me.

Visiting time arrived, as did the concerned friends and family, and from the looks on their faces, and the muttered conversations out of earshot, I realised that I was in a right pickle.

When they left I desperately wanted to leave with them, and not be stuck in this nightmare that had been thrust upon me.

Even though things looked bleak I tried to cheer myself up by telling myself that I was a winner, I was alive………not everyone has lived through a stroke.

But no matter how much I tried to find the positives there were none.

Then being typically practical I asked myself "where do you go from here?", and scenario after scenario went through my mind. All of them pictured a life that I did not want.

The one I had was perfect, a beautiful wife, a highly paid job, a lovely house and car, and holiday apartments abroad. I had lived the dream, and now was having a nightmare.

It was further compounded when I found out that as a result of the stroke I was now an epileptic.

The medical experts arrived to explain to me in detail what the stroke had done to me, and how they were going to put plans into place to aid my recovery.

I was going to need physiotherapy, speech therapy, and many other therapies to help me deal with the extensive brain damage that I had been left with.

Whilst dealing with the doctors I found out that I had also developed a stammer as a result of the stroke. Which at the time I was upset about, but I have since found out that my communication skills could have been damaged much further.

I found out that the stroke had killed off a huge part of my brain, and I was going to have to train other bits of it to take over to regain what I had lost. This brains ability to do this is what is known as neuroplasticity.

I was told that It was not easy, and it could take many hours of repetitive exercises before my brain established new ways of doing things.

The process of neuroplasticity and its affect on stroke recovery is not what this book is about, and I don't intend to expand further on it now.

What I do intend to do, if you have suffered a similar fate, is to share my recovery, and all the knowledge that I have amassed in the process, with you.

It's possible, as a consequence of your stroke, you could lose your home, your job, and that your relationship with your family may be permanently altered.

How are you going to cope with what the world has just thrown at you?

I have.

That's what this book is all about.

So where do we start?

NB: this book is aimed at the "walking wounded" stroke survivor in the UK, and not those in need of long term inpatient medical care. I have written it from the perspective of a couple, one being the survivor, the other the carer, and I apologise if this does not fit with your circumstances.

With that said I do believe that the content may be of interest to all stroke survivors and their families.

Index

7. Introduction

8. Psychological Issues

17. Medical Professionals

30. How to deal with the psychological issues

41. Employment

51. Critical illness and Income Protection insurance policies.

55. Taking private retirement pensions early, gaining access to your pension.

58. Defined benefit and defined contribution pension schemes

66. Annuities and drawdown pensions.

74. The state pension.

79. Equity release - releasing some of the equity in your property.

84. Moving house and downsizing to release funds.

87. Sale of your business.

90. Benefits available

100. TIAs and seizures

105. How to regain movement in the limbs

115. Problems in communicating, and how to overcome them

122. Restoring the family dynamic

128. Looking after yourself……….prevent it happening again!

135. Further assistance

137. Details of the author

139.Acknowledgements

Introduction

This book has been written as an aid to the stroke survivor and their family following the devastation of a stroke. It has been written by a stroke survivor who understands the impact that a stroke can have upon everything you hold dear.

In an instant, all that was taken for granted, and all plans for the future have been turned on their head. This book can not undo that instant but it does provides practical advice on how to cope with it all , both emotionally and financially.

The author's experience in finance means that you're not only getting a book which helps you deal with the problems a stroke can bring, but also covers an in-depth summary of how to deal with the financial problems a stroke can cause. The book will cover the following topics:-

Can I get my hands on my pension fund?

Which equity release plan can I use?

Should I claim Personal Independence Payment?

What other benefits can I claim?

I would advise that the family/carer reads this book first, as, if they're anything like me, the stroke survivor won't be in a fit state to read and digest its content for a while.

It may be a bit longer before they can write their own book on stroke recovery!

Psychological Issues

I'll warn you that this section does not make for cheerful reading, and it'll help if you bear in mind that you have just experienced a very serious traumatic experience that will change your life forever.

In this section I have covered the more common responses and emotions felt by stroke survivors whilst going through their stroke recovery, to give you the comfort that what you are now feeling is normal, and that it can be resolved.

Change the way you think

Let's start with the psychological issues to put you in the right frame of mind to start your new life.

The worst thing you can do at this point is to treat it as a cold, which you'll shrug off, and get back to life as you know it.

You've had a major life changing experience, and all your plans and targets may have to change.

You'll need to accept that you're not able to do all the things that you used to do, and you won't be for a while. How long will depend on you.

At first I refused to accept it and got out of my bed, and found that the damage to my legs meant I ended up in a heap on the floor. Then, after a severe reprimand from the nursing staff, I agreed to do as I was told.

There's no going back

Having a stroke is irreversible, I have found that the best way to cope with it, is to accept what has happened, and learn to enjoy my new life. (For me, this has been an enforced early retirement with my loved ones, which I find idyllic, especially when I see my former workmates continually struggling on through stress and bother).

Maybe this is not the advice that you'll want to hear at this point, and you'll create mental pictures of yourself being magically cured and completing a marathon in twelve months time. This approach is likely to lead to nothing but disappointment. Admittedly, some stroke survivors have been able to achieve remarkable things with the exceptional motivation that they have had, and maybe you're one of them. Maybe their stroke was not that severe.

You may find that you may need to reinvent yourself to cope with the different emotions that you will feel after the stroke.

It'll take a lot of hard work and commitment to recover all your abilities, and it will become a full-time battle to chip away at the disabilities you have been left with. Don't bank on being able to return to life as you knew it, you're now a completely different person, you've had your brain rewired!

The stroke can affect your self esteem, and you may start seeing yourself in a negative way, and questioning your self worth (which is a common thought process of survivors).

Even if you were a confident go-getter before the stroke it can leave you feeling vulnerable and frightened, and you shouldn't be ashamed to ask for assistance with this.

Change in personality

A stroke can cause a change in personality, which the family may find disturbing. My wife and I both agree that I have changed for the better (I don't like the person I used to be, and I'm surprised that my wife was attracted to the old me!).

I have more time now for other people, including family and friends, as my near death experience has made me re-evaluate what is important to me.

Someone's personality is a combination of their thoughts, emotions, and how they deal with their environment. These things can be changed by a stroke, which may in turn may alter your personality.

Your family need to understand these changes, as problems and activities which were once tackled easily may now become difficult or impossible for the you to do, while other things which were difficult become easier.

The family of a stroke survivor need to be aware that the survivor may become confused, unco-operative and irritable, self-centred and have frequent mood changes. They should also expect the survivor to become anxious or tearful over what appear to be trivial matters.

Emotions

There is often a loss of control over the survivors emotions, such as crying or laughing for no apparent reason, and this is called emotional liability.

The rewiring of the brain can result in a loss of control of emotions, and the family of the survivor need to be aware of this should the survivor display some inappropriate emotions at times.

The survivor may also appear apathetic or disinterested at times, but again these are common outcomes of the stroke, and they may need encouragement to go beyond the basic self-care tasks.

In addition to all the above emotions the survivor may become depressed, mourning about the loss of their previous self, and be fearful and uncertain about their future. It is not uncommon for them to see little purpose in their life, and express thoughts of death.

This depression, if left to fester, may hinder the rehabilitation process, and may need treatment, either through counselling or by way of medication.

Many stroke survivors suffer their depression in silence, and soon become accustomed to their dark view of the world.

It is important that they approach their medical advisers, and get their condition recognised in order for treatment to proceed.

Dementia

Vascular dementia is also a post-stroke problem which may affect the survivor's cognitive function or thinking abilities.

Vascular dementia makes it difficult for the survivor to process information. This can lead to memory loss, confusion, decreased attention span and problems performing everyday activities

The strokes severity and location will dictate the affect on thinking and reasoning, and the effect differs from person to person.The risk for vascular dementia increases with every stroke.

Left-hemisphere strokes are commonly associated with vascular dementia.

Symptoms of vascular dementia include:

-Memory loss

-Confusion

-Language problems (aphasia- See later notes)

-Difficulty paying attention or following a conversation

-Difficulty planning and completing tasks

-Difficulty with calculations, making decisions, solving problems

-Visual problems

-Impaired motor skills

As the symptoms of dementia due to a stroke and Alzheimer's are very similar it is very difficult to identify what is going on in recovering stroke survivors of advanced age.

The type of stroke that you've experienced will effect the seriousness of your condition, and the speed of your recovery.

But note that there's is no limit to what you can achieve, but just be realistic, and follow the advice of the professionals.

Anxiety and depression

A stroke is a sudden and devastating event that can leave you dealing with a condition similar to post traumatic stress.

Stroke survivors often suffer from anxiety and depression, and become highly emotional, so don't be surprised if you break into tears for no apparent reason.

I have, I fear the bus conductor is still shaking his head now!

Personally, I can't watch the film 'it's a wonderful life' now, without turning into a whimpering wreck.

Stroke survivors can often suffer panic attacks, and can become anxious about their finances or from suffering another stroke.

This anxiety can be exacerbated if they suffer seizures as a consequence of their stroke.

You may have concerns that you cannot get around on your own, and that your demeanour shows signs of the stroke.

This may affect your confidence and your willingness to go out and meet people.

But the more you go out the sooner you can overcome your concerns, and every trip out will strengthen you and speed your recovery.

Your confidence may also be affected in many other ways as you worry about your mobility, and your ability to deal with social events which previously caused you no concern.

You are likely to become frustrated when your body won't respond to your commands, and, sadly, this frustration is often meted out on those nearest to us, those who care.

You may not want to be treated as an invalid, and offered assistance all the time, but remember that those who are offering the help, are good intentioned, before you snap at them.

Anger and frustration

Anger is a common emotion shown by stroke survivors, and it is often, as already stated above, directed at those who care the most.

The anger comes about when the survivor feels that they have been dealt an unfair blow, which they can do little to resolve, and it can manifest itself when the simplest task cannot be performed.

I've recently come across a gentleman whose family left him as they couldn't cope with his temper following his stroke. He has learnt to curb his temper since, and, thankfully, his life is returning to normal.

Learn to look for the positive outcome that may come of your tirade, before you open your mouth. If there is none, shut up!

The stroke survivor, who was previously the breadwinner, can often feel that they have become a burden on their loved ones, and may be frustrated by their inability to remedy their situation.

It is important that the family recognise this, and don't marginalise or patronise the stroke survivor.

Who cares for the carer?

It is important for everyone to consider the effect the stroke has also had on the carer/close family member, as they may be going through a similar hell, as their plans and dreams have also been decimated.

They may have to shelve their dreams of a career to spend more time in their carers role, but they should not vent their frustration on the survivor.

They may even have to give up their employment, to become a full-time carer, which may add to the anxiety about finances.

As a result they may also feel isolated as their world is now centred around the stroke survivor.

The survivor can, at times, be overwhelmed by emotions, and despair that things may never get better.

It is often difficult to control the emotions, of feeling low, anxiety and anger, especially in the early stages of recovery, but things get better as time goes by.

In a lot of cases the emotions may never completely go away, but the survivor finds them easier to live with over time.

Will medication help?

When survivors discuss their problems with their GP's they are often given the choice of undergoing some form of cognitive behavioural therapy (more later) or medication, which in many cases can be in the form of anti-depressant drugs.

Anti - depressant drugs cannot cure the emotional problems, but can help mask the symptoms and often make life feel easier.

Summary

Above I have briefly run through the more likely emotional responses you may experience as a result of your stroke. You may experience others, not listed above, and the best way to deal with them is to talk through those emotions with your family or your GP.

If you ever find that you think you cannot cope with them, remember that there is always experienced specialist help available. No-one's expecting you to suffer in silence, other than yourself. There's no shame in asking for help, that's what it's there for.

Support groups

If you need any further information I would recommend that you contact, either, Different Strokes or the Stroke Association, who will be able to put you in touch with a support group close to you.

The benefit of joining a support group is that you get to meet others who are coping with the same problems that you are, and it provides an opportunity to socialise outside of the home, which may be beneficial for both the survivor and carer.

I have become good friends with the others in our support group, and it is encouraging to see everyone making progress in their recovery.

Specialist medical care

It is important that the psychological issues, for both parties, are addressed in the same way as the physical disabilities as part of the recovery, and the services of a neuropsychologist can be engaged at an early stage, if it is considered appropriate. Your GP or neurologist should be able to refer you to one with experience in dealing with stroke survivors and their families.

This may be the time to introduce you to the medical professionals you may need to deal with in your recovery process.

Medical professionals

If you're as lucky as I was, your recovery from your stroke will involve a team of special people with the skills and empathy to turn your life back around, some of whom will become good friends.

Neurologist

Whilst in hospital, recovering from the stroke, you will be under the care of the consultant neurologist, who, in brief, will try to determine the cause of your stroke, advise you on positive lifestyle changes, and prescribe medications to minimise any further strokes.

The consultant neurologist will be a doctor who has decided to specialise in all matters related to the brain, and will often manage a ward specifically for stroke survivors.

Neurology is the branch of medicine concerned with the study and treatment of disorders of the nervous system, which is a complex, sophisticated system that regulates and coordinates the body activities.

The central nervous system consists of the brain and spinal cord, and it is these that a neurologist focusses on, and treats disorders of, such as stroke and epilepsy.

Neurologists do not perform surgery. If one of their patients requires surgery, they refer them to a neurosurgeon.

Whilst the neurologist is treating you he/she will take a number of brain scans to assess the damage that the stroke has caused, and to monitor the recovery in progress. They will also review your cognitive and physical abilities as your recovery progresses.

He/she will advise on a course of treatment to aid recovery, and direct the team dealing with your recovery.

He/she will usually have ultimate responsibility for the care of the stroke survivors, not only on the ward but also after you have been discharged from hospital.

The team

He/she will monitor your recovery with the assistance of a team, usually made up of:-

- Occupational therapist
- Physiotherapist
- Speech therapist
- Neuropsychologist
- Stroke discharge team
- Social workers
- GP

Occupational therapist

Occupational therapists take a leading role in the early part of the stroke survivors recovery.

They assist by ensuring that that stroke survivor can relearn some basic functions in order that they can return to lead a full and independent life.

Occupational therapy is an important part of recovery and rehabilitation. It involves re-learning everyday activities to enable the stroke survivor to lead a full and independent life. It helps them regain the basic skills needed for daily tasks
Occupational therapy can help you with practical tasks such as getting out of bed, washing or making a hot drink.

Occupational therapists look at all aspects of daily life and look for practical ways you can complete your tasks.

When the occupational therapist is happy that the survivor has relearnt how to do their basic functions safely their stay in hospital may be considered to be brought to a close.

Although your first experience of occupational therapy will be in hospital, therapists can be based in other locations. These can include community rehabilitation services, social services departments, housing and mental health teams.

Your occupational therapist can help you develop your skills and confidence to manage activities that are important to your health and wellbeing.

Physiotherapist

Physiotherapists work with stroke survivors to help them regain movement in their limbs, and also provide practical advice on how to deal with their condition.

Physiotherapy helps to restore movement and function when someone is affected by injury, illness or disability.

The physiotherapist can help reverse the effects of the complete or partial paralysis caused by a stroke.

It is common that limbs fail to move in the way they did before the stroke, the affected side of the body may feel different, and certain movements become painful.

Physiotherapists help survivors deal with the above and the problems they may experience with posture and balance.

They can also advise on ways to undertake tasks to minimise the risks of falls.

The stroke can affect the arm in a way that it's weight is allowed to drag, and this can cause a partial dislocation of the shoulder (called a subluxation) which can be quite painful. Physiotherapists are aware of this and can devise a series of exercises to build up the strength in the arm again.

The work with the physiotherapists to try to regain the use of the limbs can be quite intensive, and again, to avoid disappointment, it is advisable that the goals set regarding recovery are achievable.

Given that a lot of the work in building up muscle strength in the limbs will involve training new areas of the brain to take over those functions, the physiotherapist will need a knowledge of neurophysiotherapy.

A neurophysiotherapist is trained to understand the impact of the damage to the brain and nervous system as a result of a stroke, and they can structure a specific rehabilitation program to suit.

The physiotherapy can often begin with basic exercise sessions on the ward, and can progress to more specialist sessions in a physiotherapy gymnasium.

The physiotherapists in the hospital will concentrate on building up the strength of the limbs to allow a discharge from the ward. Thereafter a community physiotherapy rehabilitation team may take over, by continuing the exercise sessions, either in the survivors own home, or at a physiotherapy gymnasium on an out-patient basis.

A common problem caused by a stroke is foot drop, where you lose the ability to lift your foot, with the result that your toes drag on the ground.

This is often rectified by intensive physiotherapy or by the use of an orthotic, called a splint, which holds the foot and ankle in place.

It is important that physiotherapy commences as early as possible after the stroke to prevent muscle tightness, that may exacerbate spasticity.

Spasticity

Spasticity is a condition in which certain muscles are continuously contracted. This contraction causes stiffness or tightness of the muscles and can interfere with normal movement, speech and gait.

Shortly after a stroke, some people experience increased muscle tone and their body posture becomes very rigid, with elbows held rigidly at the sides, wrists and fingers bent, and fists clenched.

It is not uncommon to see stroke survivors with clenched fists, and they may need to work hard at stretching their muscles to alleviate the problem.

I managed to deal with mine by laying my hand, palm facing down, flat on a surface, such as a counter, and pushing as much weight as I could down through the wrist. I will warn you that this remedy is not without pain.

When spasticity affects the legs they are usually extended at the hips and knees with the ankles and toes flexed, which may cause problems with walking.

I still have a big toe that insists on pointing skywards, but I have dealt with the situation and can walk relatively well by utilising a toe separator.

As the stroke survivor recovers with intensive physiotherapy, nerve signals that control motor functions may improve, and movement of the limbs will be improved (this is explored in greater detail later in the book).

Physiotherapy helps the control as motor functions improve, and negates the spasticity which thrives on the inactivity of the limbs.

Spasticity may be as mild as the feeling of tightness in the muscles or may be severe enough to produce painful, uncontrollable spasms in the legs and arms.

It may also create feelings of pain or tightness in and around joints and can cause lower back pain.

It is mostly caused by damage to the portion of the brain that controls voluntary movement. Your physical disability is basically due to your brain losing it's connection with your muscles, you need to retrain it (as if you were an infant!).

Speech therapist

A speech therapist may be needed if the stroke has affected that part of the brain that deals with language, and understanding.

Often, one of the most frustrating outcomes of a stroke is that the stroke survivor cannot find the words that they want to say, and may often, as a consequence, feel that they should give up midway through their sentences.

If you experience this, don't worry, it's fairly normal, and there are specialists who can help with this condition.

This condition is called anomia, which is often covered under the badge of aphasia, which is the inability to comprehend or formulate language. It can affect auditory comprehension, verbal expression, reading and writing, and functional communication.

Aphasia can have a major effect on the stroke survivor's self confidence as they are unable to communicate without assistance. Mercifully, most survivors see improvement in their condition within two to three months of their stroke.

Another possible outcome is one that affected me personally, a stutter. I managed to deal with this problem after a couple of visits to a speech therapist.

Neuropsychologist

The neuropsychologist is specially trained to understand the relationship between the brain and neuropsychological function, and they require not only a knowledge of the broad range of mental health problems, but also specialist knowledge in the neurosciences.

We have already looked at how a stroke can affect the way a person thinks, feels and behaves. It is the neuropsychologist's job to assess and help to treat the effects of these problems.

They do this by an evaluation which can include an interview and questions that will help outline your performance of daily tasks, as well as identifying memory issues and mental health concerns.

The evaluation will also cover information on symptoms, medical history, and the medications you take.

During the interview there will usually be a set of standardised tests to measure your brain function, including:

-memory

-cognitive ability

-personality

-problem-solving

-reasoning

-emotions

Following your evaluation the neuropsychologist will compare your test results with other stroke survivors and of other people with a similar education and age.

They then may, if they consider it appropriate, instigate a treatment plan which may include medication, rehabilitation therapy, or, in extreme cases, surgery.

The Stroke Discharge Team

The Stroke Discharge team is usually made up all the therapists above working together to ensure a full a recovery as they consider possible. The extent of this recovery will vary, as it will be dependent upon the severity of the stroke and the personality of the survivor.

The team will work together with the survivor, and their carer/family to ensure a discharge from hospital to a safe home environment, ensuring that mobility aids are available where necessary.

They can provide daily (if deemed necessary) stroke rehabilitation in the home and the community, and advise on stroke recovery generally.

They will work until they are satisfied that the survivor is able to safely manage with their condition in the long term.

Social worker

The hospital based social workers, who are often employed by the local authority, undertake a similar role as that of the occupational therapist, but on a more practical basis. Their role can include the following:-

-Putting together a care package, and arranging help with the preparation of meals etc.

-Provide assistance to the survivor if they are entitled to any benefits, and assist in making claims on their behalf.

Often, if the survivor has very simple care needs, a social worker may not be involved, and the occupational therapist or community care or social work assistant may provide the back-up.

The amount of back-up will depend upon the severity of the stroke, and the domestic arrangements of the survivor.

Leaving hospital

Following an assessment (including finances) a decision may be made whether the survivor will be eligible for a free personal care payment, and whether they can return home with a care package or whether their needs can be better met in a care home.

The free personal care element may often be paid directly to a care home if it is thought that the survivor can be better cared for there.

To allay your fear that you'll end up in a care home I would like to add that this option is often only considered in the event of an elderly or vulnerable patient, or when the stroke has been severe.

If it is considered that the survivor is unable to return home safely, the social worker may help them to look at options for alternative accommodation, such as adapted housing or care homes.

Assessment of needs

As part of the decision process to decide where the survivor will reside, the social worker will carry out a care needs assessment for the survivor, and may also carry out a care needs assessment for the carer.

A financial assessment is also often undertaken because some of the services may be means tested (the cost you pay may depend on your ability to pay, which is calculated using the level of the survivors (and family's) savings and income etc.) More on this later (in the finances section).

Some services may be free depending on the survivors circumstances.

The survivor, and their family are free to arrange their own care, and the social worker can give advice on this, and supply a list of private care agencies. This is known as self directed support.

The care packages, and the payment thereof, may vary as each survivors needs will differ.

General Practitioner (GP)

The stroke survivors doctor (general practitioner) will generally be involved with strokes in one of three ways:-

-advising patients on lifestyle changes, and prescribing medications to reduce the likelihood of stroke. This prevention role is very important and is gaining more prevalence in healthcare planning in general.

It has been estimated, in the U.K., that Around 7,000 strokes each year are being prevented thanks to GPs more than doubling the number of patients at high risk, being prescribed with drugs to prevent blood clotting.

-providing immediate medical care, in the event of them being on hand when someone suffers a stroke, and ensuring that the survivors time, upon arrival at a hospital, with the capacity to deliver thrombolysis, is minimised.

-providing medical care, advice and medication to survivors post stroke, and adhering to the neurologists care plan. As the survivor's health in general will be poor following the stroke the GP may initiate more preventative measures, such as flu vaccinations, to ensure the survivors wellbeing.

I have briefly referred to thrombolysis above, so maybe this is the best place to explain more about the stroke you have experienced.

If the stroke is caused by a blood clot (ischaemic stroke), the survivor will be treated with a clot-busting drug to try to disperse the clot and return the blood supply to their brain.

This treatment is known as thrombolysis, and it needs to be administered within four and a half hours of the stroke to minimise the long term effects of the stroke. For smaller clots thrombolysis involves administering A tPA (tissue plasminogen activator) via an IV in the arm, which helps dissolve the clot.

For larger ones there is a minimally invasive procedure known as a thrombectomy, where a stent retriever is routed up to the brain to remove the clot.

(Given the government's chronic underfunding of our medical services some stroke survivors are being forced to wait in A & E departments on stretchers for up to seventeen hours before a doctor can see them!)

Alternative treatment will be necessary if the stroke has been caused by a bleed (haemorrhagic).

It is very important that a CT scan of the brain is taken to determine what kind of stroke has occurred.

The diagnosis is key to starting a speedy treatment to curb the blockage or stop the bleeding, and as the treatment for the two is so opposite a correct diagnosis is essential.

What is an ischemic stroke?

There are two major types of ischemic stroke:

-Thrombotic strokes are caused when a blood clot forms in an artery leading to the brain.

-Embolic strokes begin with a clot forming elsewhere in the body, that breaks loose and travels to the brain.

These two types of stroke account for about 85% of all cases.

The symptoms shown by those experiencing such a stroke are numbness or weakness on one side of the body or face, trouble speaking and difficulty with vision or balance.

What is hemorrhagic stroke?

A hemorrhagic stroke occurs when a weak blood vessel bursts and bleeds into the brain.

The symptoms of this type of stroke are similar to those above, but there may also be a sudden onset headache or head pain.

Hemorrhagic strokes are less common than ischemic strokes, only accounting for about 15 percent of all stroke cases, but they do lead to more fatalities.

They are usually remedied by a surgical clip being placed at the base of the brain to remove blood flow and stop the bleeding. This is known as clipping. A craniotomy, which involves removing a portion of the skull to access the brain is necessary for this procedure.

An option to the above is coiling, which involves guiding a coil up through an artery in the body into the brain, where the coils are detached and are put in place to reduce the bloodflow.

Summary

So now you've been introduce to the team, and know more about your stroke, when someone comes along and prods you, talking medical gobbledygook, you should have a good idea who they are, and what they're talking about.

How to deal with the psychological issues

Earlier we looked at the more common emotions experienced by stroke survivors. In this chapter we're going to look at ways of positively dealing with these emotions, and practical ways to cope with stroke.

Don't worry

I know the whole experience is an ordeal, but try not let it get you down and turn you into a negative person. There's better to come.

We've all got worries, and we all cope with them, so let's not waste time on them. We can't see the future, so why waste time worrying about it. Whatever happens we can cope with it.

Worrying is just seeing the future with a negative outcome. Are you a clairvoyant? Things may turn out alright!

If you are worried about your finances please note I had my stroke over eight years ago and I've not gone bust yet. I'm sure you'll find a way to cope like I have, a smaller car or the bus, and introduce yourself to Aldi.

I wasted a lot of time worrying about money.

Worrying can have a negative effect on your body, and your outlook on life, and ultimately your health.

Reject your negative thoughts

You might feel down and dejected at the moment. But if you let those negative feelings take hold they can ruin your life.

Those emotions can lead to self-judgment and self-criticism, frustration, and even jealousy of others.

All of those negative feelings can lead to emotions like resentment and anger. In some cases, they can even lead to feelings of anxiety and depression.

Learn to turn cant's into cans. Rather than focusing on what you can't do concentrate more on what you can, if it's more than it was yesterday you're making progress.

You've got to learn to recognise when you're having a negative thought, ask yourself why, and tell yourself off. The more you do this the less of them you'll have.

Don't give up, you can still achieve things with your life, just look at alternative ways of doing them.

You can chip away at the negatives, a little at a time, even if it's only slightly moving a finger or a toe. Set yourself achievable goals on your way to recovery, and reward yourself with a treat whenever you achieve a milestone.

Be bold

It is important to get out and about as soon as you can, as every trip makes you stronger.

I, personally, would always seek the most difficult way to do things, from finding the most uneven ground to walk on, to seeking the least welcoming person to ask questions to.

I found that this approach hardened me and made tasks easier.

Don't get depressed, it's happened, there's nothing you can do about it. Learn to accept your situation, cheer up and get on with life. Make the most of what you've got.

There's no-one to blame, and there's no point in trying to apportion it to anyone or thing.

Draw yourself up a personal balance sheet, listing the good things and the bad things about your life. Your family should be very high up on that list. Don't discount yourself and your achievements.

A good exercise to remedy your face drop is to practice smiling in a mirror. It's hard to be down with a smile on your face, and you can't fail to amuse yourself pulling faces, which is a good exercise to correct your face drop.

Bear in mind that you've experienced a random negative event, and that there's no harm in wishing for a random positive event, as anything can happen.

Don't be so cruel to yourself, you wouldn't to anyone else. So stop putting yourself through hell, and ask yourself why you're doing it. The effect of you answering back those negative emotions can be amazing.

If you let the negativity take hold you'll become governed by the 'whirlpool of despair' (my description). This is when a negative thought becomes a worry which turns into anxiety, and then panic, and an avalanche of uncontrolled emotions.

I can give you an example of this below.

It is a glorious summers night and your daughter is a little late coming home from school, other than that everything is wonderful. You suddenly have the thought that the road opposite the school, which your daughter has to cross to catch her bus, is very busy.

It's that time of night when the sun is low in the sky, and can blind one as they are driving. You instantly worry that your daughter could get knocked down by a driver unable to see her in the glare of the sun.

It's not like her to be this late, and you become anxious that something terrible has happened to her, and picture her lying on the road.

Then you hear the siren of an emergency vehicle, and assume the worse, and panic, with pictures of the carnage racing through your mind.

A minute later the doorbell rings, and you fear the worst, and race through the house expecting to be shortly comforted by a policeman.

Instead, you are confronted by Mr. Middleton, the father of Pippa, your daughter's best friend, and by his side is your daughter, with the biggest smile on her face.

You are so relieved that you barely hear his tale regarding Pippa's new horse, and the two girls riding it around the paddock. He had realised it had got late, and had given her a lift home, but they were held up by a police car on an emergency.

Then you hear your daughter say "I've had the best time ever!" So could you have had too, if it hadn't been for the chain of negative thoughts that had resulted in the panic you had needlessly put yourself through.

You could have been sat on your back terrace, with a gin and tonic, watching the (offending) sun go down over the trees at the bottom of your garden.

But now you are going to spend the rest of the evening researching how much it costs to own a horse!

The above shows that it is not life's events that govern our behaviour, but how we react to them. Make your life better by thinking positively. Don't waste it by making up negative scenarios.

ANT's and dealing with them

The American psychiatrist Daniel G Amen refers to ANT's in his book ' Change your brain, change your life', and defines them as Automatic Negative Thoughts. The book describes ways to deal with them as part of a rehabilitation process.

Key to dealing with them is being aware that you are having them, and immediately over-riding them.

He advises that we learn to overcome the tendency toward pessimistic predictions and that this is essential to bringing peace to ones life.

He also advises that pessimists die earlier as the constant stress from negative predictions lowers the immune system's effectiveness and increases the risk of becoming ill.

Your thoughts affect every cell in your body. Learning how to kill the fortune-telling ANTs that go through your mind is essential to effectively dealing with the anxiety generated in the brain.

" Do not accept every thought that comes into your mind. Thoughts are just thoughts, not facts."

Support Groups

I have already run through the benefits of joining a support group, but it is important to find one with other survivors of similar age and motivation.

The Different strokes groups are more focussed on the younger/more active stroke survivor.

There's nothing more demotivating than joining a group who are happy to remain in their chairs for the rest of their lives.

Join a support group and talk things through with others who have been through the same thing.

The support group can also provide both the survivor and the carer with the opportunity to socialise outside of the family unit for the first time.

You can compare yourself to others in the support group to help measure the stage of your recovery, and your and their progress.

Interests and volunteering

Take up an interest or hobby which you can get engrossed in, to take away your thoughts from the negative.

I've developed an interest for sitting idly in Garden Centres drinking tea for most of the day.

Volunteering and assisting others can have a positive effect in the rehabilitation process.

There are many charities desperate for the help you could provide. Pick your favourite, you'll be surprised how useful you'll become.

Coping strategies

Learn cognitive behaviour therapy methods from your therapists to help you cope with panic and anxiety attacks.

I learnt a basic relaxed breathing exercise which I found very helpful in times of stress and panic. It involves taking a long inhalation through the nose for four seconds, holding it in for four seconds, and exhaling through the mouth for four seconds.

Breathing correctly

Do you breathe mostly with your chest or with your belly? Research has shown that the way you breathe has a huge impact on how you feel.

Infants and young animals breathe mostly with their bellies. They move their upper chest very little in breathing.

Yet most adults breathe almost totally from the upper part of their chest and this is not conducive to relaxation.

You can correct this negative breathing pattern, by lying on your back and placing a small book on your belly. When you breathe in, make the book go up, and when you breathe out, make the book go down.

This shifts the centre of your breathing lower in your body will help you feel more relaxed and in better control of yourself.

I would recommend that you practice this diaphragmatic breathing pattern several times a day to help you develop a deeper sense of calm and peace.

It is important to concentrate on the inhalation filling your lungs, and likewise on the exhalation.

I found the concentration, and counting involved in the above process, helped to clear my thoughts, and broke the feeling of panic.

There are many different breathing techniques, and you should try them until you find one that works for you.

Other therapies and strategies

There is also a talking therapy available, where the survivor talks through their worries with a therapist, which may help the survivor manage their problems by changing the way they think and behave.

This therapy is based on the concept that your thoughts, feelings, physical sensations and actions are interconnected, and that negative thoughts and feelings can trap you in a vicious cycle (see above).

At one stage I engaged the services of a hypnotist to help with my anxiety issues, and once he had me in a relaxed state he had me imagine a trip through a wonderful garden

I still imagine the trip through that garden in times of stress. I find that it is effective in dealing with negative thoughts.

You may of heard of mindfulness and, like me, thought of hippies, but there are some mindfulness techniques which can help in times of anxiety. One in particular is very helpful in achieving a relaxed state, it is often called the body scan.

The body scan

The body scan involves you concentrating on (contracting and) relaxing one muscle group at a time, starting with your feet, and working up until your whole body is in a state of relaxation.

There are many YouTube videos available that run through this, and other similar techniques, and you should be able to find a mindfulness group near to where you live.

When you're going through a real dark patch always remember that there's someone worse off than you, and they're coping with it.

Exercise is not only essential as part of the physical recovery but it is also very good at lifting the spirit.

The power of positive affirmations

Above we have looked at the benefits of ignoring and discounting negative thoughts. If we go one further we can look at the benefits of adopting a positive way of looking at the future.

Anything you wish to happen can happen as long as it is within your control. For example, if you wish for a job you can get one, it might take 100 applications, and 15 interviews, but in the end you will get one if you stick at it.

You need to believe it will really happen, and not get deflated at every obstacle that is put in your way.

I have always recalled the tale of the businessman who was told that one in twenty people he approached would become customers, so he adopted the approach of counting the rejections, and viewing them as steps towards his goal.

After his first rejection he worked on the premise that he had eighteen more to go before he got some business.

He couldn't get out of bed soon enough to see as many people as he could, but it soon became apparent that the estimates he had been given were wrong, and he was gaining more business than had hoped for.

If he hadn't had the positive attitude to see as many new customers this may not have happened.

You need to believe that your health will get better, and every time you have a thought telling you that it is not going to happen, ask yourself why you are thinking that way, and stick to your belief that it will happen.

Don't let others tell you that you are misinformed or deluded, but carry on believing in the targets that you have set yourself.

Write down a realistic goal for yourself and believe you're going to achieve it.

If it's within your control you will. The psychological effect of you believing in a positive outcome will alter your behaviour and make it happen. It's the exact opposite of the whirlpool of despair (above).

Summary

Most importantly, to make life easier for everyone, tell your loved ones how you feel, and listen to how they're going through an ordeal themselves.

Work more as a family unit to get through this, it will bring you closer together.

Employment

This section will deal solely with employment and the options for employees, the way the self- employed are affected will be dealt with briefly in the Finances section.

How long will I be away from work?

How long will I be off work? This will depend upon the severity of your stroke, and your ability to deal with returning to the work environment. I'll not kid you, it may be a long time, and you may never return to work.

You're not indispensable, your business will carry on, things will still get done………..so don't stress yourself thinking that you need to get back to work as soon as possible.

I understand that financial pressures may necessitate an early return to work, but most people (except bankers and insurers!) are compassionate when they are informed of a serious illness being the cause of financial pressures.

Legal rights and Reasonable Adjustment

You have got legal rights which rule that your employer has a duty to make 'reasonable adjustments' for employees who are disabled under the Equality Act 2010. You need to ensure that your employer now knows that you are disabled, and seriously ill and needing time off.

And you need to keep in touch with your employer to update them of progress.

Reasonable adjustment has not been specifically defined, so it is up to you negotiate with your employer regarding your absence from the workplace, and what will constitute your job upon your return.

How reasonable an employer will be can vary significantly, given your employment record, and their finances.

The duty to make reasonable adjustments only applies when someone has a disability as defined in the Equality Act. It does not apply if the employer could not reasonably be expected to know that a person is disabled. So let them know you are, following your stroke.

It is therefore very important to be honest about the effects of your stroke and keep in contact with your employer. The way your stroke affects your work should be documented and reviewed regularly.

How long it will take you to get back to work will depend on the effects of your stroke, the rehabilitation you have received, what work you do and the amount of support your employer is willing to give you.

No two strokes are the same. Those who experience a mild stroke could return to work within a week or two, while others may return after months or a couple of years. Some never. There's no set pattern.

Effects of the stroke

You may find that your cognitive and physical abilities are not what they were before the stroke, and that you may struggle with your job.

Fatigue is a big issue with stroke survivors, and you may not be able to cope with work at the same level as you did before the stroke.

Formulate a plan for a return to work

It is important that you discuss your stroke with your employer, and agree a plan for a manageable return to work, or possibly a new position within the business that is more suited to your new abilities.

I would recommend that, after discussions with your medical advisors, you contact your employer to try to arrange a manageable, staged return to work.

It is important, should a return to work be the plan, that you keep in touch with your employer, and update them of your progress.

Many employers will be supportive of your return to work, as if they have to replace you, they will incur recruitment and training costs.

There are some employers are are not compassionate when it comes to their employees ill-health, but thankfully these are few and far between. Most will see the benefit in retaining their staff, and will work with them to facilitate a successful return to work.

Your employer has a legal responsibility to do all they can to ensure that your stroke does not stop you from keeping your job, or having the same rights and access to opportunities that you had before.

Return to work

Even when you return to work your troubles are not entirely over, as being back in work after a long time off can be difficult, no matter how well-prepared you feel before you go back.

You may find that tasks that were easy before the stroke have become more difficult, and that regaining skills, confidence and stamina can take a long time. But don't give yourself a hard time as no-one will be expecting an instant fix, and neither should you.

Once you get back to work you will need to ensure that there is a regular review plan put in place in order that both you and your employer can assess your performance, and adjust the tasks/hours of work etc. as necessary.

Leave policy

Some employers have a disability leave policy which allows employees to take paid leave related to their disability, such as for treatment or rehabilitation.

This is often separate from sickness absence. Disability leave is treated as a reasonable adjustment under the Equality Act, but employers are not obliged to offer it.

If disability leave is not available in your workplace, time off for medical appointments may be considered a reasonable adjustment.

Statutory Sick Pay

You can check with your employer what their policy is on sick pay during sickness absence. Not all businesses offer their own sick pay benefits and some provide Statutory Sick Pay only. Statutory Sick Pay is the basic level of sick pay set by the UK Government.

You can get a maximum of £92.05 a week Statutory Sick Pay (SSP) for up to 28 weeks.

Don't focus on the 28 weeks and make it a target, you could put yourself under tremendous pressure, and in danger of another stroke if you do.

I realise that the bills won't pay themselves and we'll look further at how you can relieve the financial pressures, and negate the need for an early return to work, in the next section.

Retirement

It may be that both you and your employer will agree that you are no longer able to do the job you used to do, and an alternative position, or retirement, may be offered.

I managed to negotiate an acceptable financial package when, both I and my workplace, agreed that I no longer had the cognitive ability to do my job.

Admittedly, it was a big blow at the time, and it took a long time for me to adjust to an early retirement.

Dismissal

If the survivors condition does not improve can they be dismissed for taking long-term sick leave?

Yes, employers can dismiss employees for extended absence due to long-term ill health.

But first the employer has to prove that they have explored all avenues to help their employee get back to work.

If the employer decides to pursue an ill-health dismissal, they need to prove that no reasonable adjustments can be made to enable the employee to do their job.

Unfair dismissal

If the employer does not explore all reasonable adjustments, and then dismisses the employee, an unfair dismissal has taken place.

The employee may then be able to bring a claim for unfair dismissal. If this occurs to you, you should seek advice urgently from a solicitor or the Citizens Advice, as there is a time limit within which to make a claim.

If the employer does not want the hassle of an unfair dismissal claim they may try to take an alternative action, that of making the role redundant. But you cannot be selected for redundancy based on your disability. This again could be grounds for unfair dismissal.

Early retirement options

It may be that your finances will allow you to take an early retirement, especially if the employment could have been partly responsible for the stroke. If this is the case the employer may be more generous with its parting settlement!

Once your employer realises the extent of the damage of the stroke they may be keen to negotiate an early retirement with you. I would highly recommend legal advice is taken, (or contact Citizens Advice), if this course of action is being considered.

The decision to retire cannot be taken lightly, and all your pension/income options need to be explored first with a financial adviser. The minefield of private and state pensions, and annuities will be explored further in the book.

A retirement could prove more conducive to your rehabilitation as it removes the time pressures that come with a return to work.

A retirement also gives you the opportunity to look at other options, if you feel you are ready for a change, and not ready to sit back and retire to the garden yet.

You could try a new career or volunteering, the world's your oyster! There are plenty of opportunities and retraining courses available.

I undertook an online Open University course on Investment Planning, and decided to write a few books, similar to this one.

There's nothing stopping you doing anything, but the market for lame trapeze artists is very limited!

Even if your present employer writes you off there are plenty of other businesses that are willing to take a gamble on disabled employees, in fact there is legislation which actively encourages it.

The two ticks symbol

The two ticks system may help you if you are considering another job, if your finances make this a necessity.

If you find a Two Ticks symbol on a job advert it means that the employer is taking positive steps to employ disabled people. Employers who display this symbol are committed to interview all applicants with a disability who meet the minimum criteria for a job vacancy.

If you apply for a job when this symbol has been displayed you will be considered on your own abilities. The symbol also means that the employer has promised to support people with disabilities in the workplace.

Most workplaces have been adapted to accommodate the disabled. Times have changed since I worked with a man confined to a wheelchair, who was forced to ascend and descend a set of stairs on his bottom everyday in order to get to and from work.

Company in-house sickness schemes

Some employers have their own insurance schemes to cover sickness. You may find, by default, that you have been paying into one of these. The employer will advise on the level of cover, and how you can make a claim.

Others offer a sick pay which may reduce over time, depending on your contract and how long you have been an employee.

Insurances

You may be lucky enough to find that you've been paying an insurance policy (by default) to cover the position you are in, which may ease your worries about employment.

There are insurance policies which pay out either a tax free lump sum or a fixed regular amount until retirement date for those who are diagnosed or suffer from a serious illness.

These insurance policies, sometimes called critical illness or income protection policies, are often included in things like bank account packages that you may have signed up to, and you may have been unaware of the cover that you have had.

I will explore these insurances further in the finance section.

Summary

With the help of your employer, family and understanding of your creditors, and not to mention claiming the benefits that are due to you (see later notes), you may be able to delay your return to work, and concentrate more on your recovery.

Employment Reference sources

For more information regarding your rights at work I suggest that you look on the Equality and Human Rights Commission website: www.equalityhumanrights.com

In order to help stroke survivors in their quest to return to work the Stroke Association has issued 'A complete guide to stroke for employers', which lists tips to help employers deal with stroke survivors returning to work.

The Stroke Association has also produced a guide for employees, 'A complete guide to work and stroke', which aims to provide you with all the information you need to think about your return to work after a stroke. It provides information on disability rights at work, and tips for career-changers. The guide also gives tips on planning your return to work when you feel ready.

Even if you do not think of yourself as disabled, the information in the guide may still apply to you. You might still be eligible for support even if you have made a good recovery.

You may have returned to work and received little support so far. The guide will help you to understand what support is available and how to get it.

The charity, Different Strokes, has issued a leaflet 'Benefits and financial assistance' which covers this topic also.

Critical illness and Income Protection insurance policies.

As a consequence of the stroke your household finances will have most likely suffered significantly, and you will be desperate to remedy the situation.

I would urge that you look at your insurance policies to check whether your predicament is covered by a policy that you are already paying.

I don't want to raise your hopes too high but Critical illness cover, in particular, has often been tagged onto other financial products, such as a life insurance policy, in the past.

Critical illness insurance policies

If I'm having to explain to you what a critical illness insurance policy is for the first time, horse and bolted come to mind. But you may have, inadvertently, been covered by one and the eagerness of insurance salesmen, in the past, to maximise their commissions, may have resulted in you having this cover.

Critical illness cover is a form of insurance which pays out a tax-free lump sum in the event that you are diagnosed with a specified illness or medical condition during the term of the policy.

There are 36 specified illnesses and deceases covered by all these policies, one of which is stroke, so if you find you have a critical illness policy you should be covered.

A lot of life insurance policies include a critical illness cover, so it may be worth looking at your life cover to check whether you are due anything.

You probably took a life cover out when you took on your mortgage, and at that time the thought of a critical illness could not have been further from your mind.

If you are self employed you may have an insurance policy, as part of your banking arrangements.

I've just been online and got quotes for 25 years for a life insurance policy for £300,000 for a 29 year old, with a critical illness addition of £100,000, and one of £300,000, without any critical illness cover.

The first quote was for £27.24/month, and the second was for £10.01/month, so by default I calculate the cost of £100,000 of critical illness cover to be £17.23/month.

I had to mislead the comparison website that I was much younger to get the quotes above.

The payouts from critical illness policies can be quite significant so if you do fail to check for cover you do so at your peril.

I used my critical illness insurance payout to pay off my immediate debts and keep the wolf from the door!

Income protection policies

Income protection policies provide a fixed level of income in the event that you are diagnosed with a specified illness or medical condition during the term of the policy. Again, most policies will usually provide for stroke.

These policies will provide an income you can rely on, that will not vary, unless it is linked to the level of inflation (when it will increase in your favour each year).

The amount paid out is usually dependent upon the level of earnings at the date that the policy was initiated.

An accident and sickness policy paying out £1,500/month to a 29 year old costs at the moment (October 2018), £16.35/month.

The benefits are usually paid up to the age of 60, and may continue to be paid out even if you return to work at a reduced salary.

I would have been lost had it not been for the income from my income protection policy.

Some insurance policies for the self employed will provide for sufficient income to keep the business running, by covering overheads and staff costs. But often the business can suffer without the participation and drive of the proprietor.

Unfortunately many businesses fail when the proprietor suffers a serious illness, due to them running out of cash. In hindsight, it is easy to agree that everyone should have some sort of sickness insurance.

It has been surprisingly difficult for insurance companies to sell these policies, to both the employed and self-employed, given the incidence of serious illness in society today.

Employed stroke survivors have a tendency to deal with this episode better than their self-employed counterparts, as the employed tend to have a lot of financial back up through their employment, and the self-employed are notoriously bad at providing for themselves in times of need.

In particular the self-employed continue to fail to provide for themselves. The self-employed are not very good at providing for illness or their retirement. The figures below show this clearly.

Forty-three per cent of self-employed workers do not have a pension.

Thirty-six per cent say they cannot afford to save into a pension.

Thirty-one per cent will depend upon the state pension to support their retirement. I fear that the country is heading for a big financial black hole when the proverbial hits the fan!

The expansion of the Gig economy (where employees are encouraged to take on self-employed positions, often losing their employment benefits) has exacerbated this situation.

Regarding the finance detail, above and elsewhere in this book, I have provided you with generic guidance but I do stress that before you take any action you take independent advice regarding your individual circumstances.

Taking private retirement pensions early, gaining access to your pension.

The monies invested into personal pensions can normally only be accessed from the age of 55, either through an annuity or by way of income drawdown, (often with an option to take up to 25% of the pension fund tax free).

(The distinction between annuity and drawdown will be explained further below).

So, it appears that only stroke survivors over the age of 55 can access part of their pension to help them sort out their finances. But there is also the opportunity for stroke survivors younger than 55 to access those funds also.

Early payout of pensions under ill – health provisions

A number of private pension policies do allow for an earlier payout when the policy holder becomes ill.

Being allowed to draw the benefits early on the grounds of ill- health should enable you to enjoy the scheme benefits that are outlined in the scheme rules, which in some cases can include 25% of the fund tax free.

The disadvantage to taking the pension early is that it hasn't had the time to reach its true potential, and the fund will be a lot lower than it would have been had it run its full course.

Whether you can do this will depend on your pension scheme and their definition of what ill health might be. Normally, the usual definition is where "your physical or mental health is bad enough to stop you from carrying on working, or which seriously reduces the amount you can earn."

Providing you meet the criteria of your scheme, you may be able to take your benefits early – and your scheme may also pay you an ill health pension due to your condition. But this will depend on the policy you have.

There are two sets of regulations you'll have to satisfy if a disability stops you working and you need early access to your pension.

The first of these has been set by the tax man and it states:

-You must be incapable of working as a result of physical or mental impairment.

-You've had to cease working due to that disability.

-You're not capable of returning to your job in the future.

Medical evidence needs to be provided which validates the above.

The second set of rules will usually be set by the individual pension provider. The rules may vary as each pension provider will have their own set of rules.

For example, some pension plans let you retire early if you're incapable of fulfilling your role. But there are other plans that require you to be incapable of doing any other job, before you get access to your pension.

Again detailed medical evidence from your GP and an independent medical advisor will be needed.

Payout of pension to terminally ill policy holders

If your circumstances are more immediate, you may be entitled to more access to your pension benefits. For example, if you're diagnosed with a very serious or terminal condition, where your life expectancy is determined to be less than 12 months, you may be able to take the whole of your pension pot as a lump sum, although special tax rules may apply.

As you would expect the detail that you need to provide to the pension provider to make a claim is quite significant.

But as any payment from the fund means that there is less time for your pension pot to grow, some pension providers may reduce the pension that you will get. Many schemes however will make no such reduction.

Others may actually increase the pension if, for example, in the case of a terminal condition, it is unlikely that you will be claiming your pension for a long period.

Because schemes can have such different rules, its really important that you talk to your pension provider as soon as possible. They should be able to provide you with further information about your policy's rules.

The pension reforms in 2016 removed the need for pensioners to buy an annuity to provide income until they die (which we are yet to look at), and give them access to effectively do what they want with their pension funds.

This flexibility is very useful for stroke survivors trying to make the most out of the early access to their pension funds.

Defined benefit and defined contribution pension schemes

The flexibility (discussed above) only applies to those pensions which most individuals will have taken out privately, called 'defined contribution' pensions which will usually provide a lump sum upon maturity.

(They are described as defined contribution pensions as only the payments into the scheme (the contributions) have been defined.)

It doesn't apply to those with more generous and guaranteed final salary pensions (or defined benefit pensions), which are usually provided by employers.

(These are described as defined benefit pensions as only the level of pension, e.g. 50% of final salary,(the benefit) has been defined).

Whilst the pension freedoms apply to those with defined contribution pensions those with final salary (defined benefit pensions) are in a less advantageous situation. Although it could be argued that their pensions tend to be better than defined contribution pensions.

Defined contribution pension schemes, take contributions and invest them to provide a pot of money for the pensioner at retirement. As we have seen, the pensioner can effectively do what he wants with this money to provide for his future.

When the policy holder of a defined contribution scheme retires the amount of his pot that is still invested may increase in value with positive investment returns, which may result in a bigger pension.

Whereas once you retire on a final salary scheme the pension you will receive cannot be affected by positive or negative movements in investments.

25% tax free lump sum from defined contribution schemes

Under UK law, a person can access up to 25% of their defined contribution fund tax free from the age of 55, or earlier if the ill-health provisions apply.

(Please note that this applies to defined contribution pensions only, defined benefit pension schemes will have their own rules)

The ability to access the pension, and, more importantly, the 25% tax free lump sum could be critical to a number of stroke survivors.

With the average pension fund being £106,000, the tax free lump sum of £26,500 can prove a useful addition to shore up the household finances.

But if the finances are not that tight there is always the option to leave the pension pot intact, and not take the lump sum, and leave your pension to continue growing (to provide a higher income over the course of retirement).

25% of the pension pot will still remain tax free if you wish to draw down the amount gradually over a number of years, (unless the government change the rules), so at the moment there is no compulsion to withdraw 25% as a tax free lump sum.

But many prefer to take the lump sum with plans to invest it in a bank account, take an extravagant holiday, buy an investment property, or clear some debts.

If you wish to pay some debts off by way of a 25% payout from your pension, and the amount that you need is less than 25% of the value of the pension, the calculation of the further amounts you can take from the fund tax free get very complicated.

If 25% of your pension fund is not enough to sort out your financial difficulties there are other options available to you.

All pensioners should bear in mind that any money not withdrawn, upon retirement, will carry on growing or could fall in value.

Retirees need to think carefully when deciding whether to take their maximum tax-free cash lump sum immediately or leave more of their money invested.

For some the cash received is vital to clear debts, perhaps pay off a mortgage or clear a credit card. However, not everyone needs it as soon as they retire and the money left invested in the pension may continue to grow tax-free.

There are four ways of extracting the money from your defined contribution pension:

-Take the 25% tax free cash only.

You can keep the balance of the money invested in your defined contribution pension and benefit that the remaining money will gain from any investment returns before you take it.

You need to take this option before you move the balance of your pension into an annuity or income drawdown (more later).

-Take all of your pension fund including the tax free cash

Only 25% of the amount withdrawn will be tax free and you will have to pay tax on the rest, this could result in part of the amount being taken being taxed at a higher rate of income tax.

If you take all your pension in one go you need to consider whether you can somehow find another way to provide an income as you grow older. However, if you need the cash, and have retirement income from other sources, this may work for you.

-Only take part of the tax free cash

As already mentioned above, this option may complicate the tax position on further withdrawals.

-Take a lump sum including tax free amount

Here 25% of the amount you withdraw is tax free and the remaining 75% is subject to income tax. You can take this type of lump sum as a one-off or a series of payments. By taking a pension lump sum and leaving the rest of your pension within the fund, you may still have unused tax free cash to take in the future. This will enable you to spread the tax free benefit over several payments.

But there are tax implications to leaving the pension pot invested.

If death occurs before age of 75 the pension pot can be passed on tax-free, whilst if over age 75, tax is paid by whoever inherits it.

Payouts from defined benefit schemes

Employees who have invested in their employers pension scheme are not able to enjoy the benefits above, but are subject to the rules of the scheme they are contributing to.

As already indicated, above, the work schemes that employees often join are referred to as defined benefit pensions.

The more generous defined benefit or final salary pensions, provide a guaranteed income after retirement until the pensioner dies.

But they rely upon the employer investing the amounts into separate pension accounts on the pensioners behalf, which has proved not to be the case in a couple of recent high profile bankruptcies.

As each scheme is different, and the agreed percentage of final salary that the pension will pay may vary, the tax-free lump sum offers made by final salary schemes upon

retirement can vary widely, and you need to take this into account.

Usually you are allowed to take anything up to 25 per cent tax-free. This may depend upon the investment prowess of the schemes administrators. As a rule the bigger the lump sum you withdraw, the more future pension you sacrifice, most schemes operate a commutation factor to calculate the amounts, with some schemes charging more for the lump sum than others.

This usually operates as follows. You might be offered £14 in the form of a lump sum for every one pound of future pension you give up. This is a commutation factor of

14:1. Other schemes may offer £18 of lump sum for every pound of pension income you sacrifice, which is a far more favourable rate of 18:1.

In terms of deciding whether a commutation offer you have received is any good, the current rates are somewhere between 15:1 to 20:1.

But can you do anything about the rate you're being offered? How does it compare with current annuity rates? It's very easy to check whether you're getting a good deal or not, many pensioners aren't! I have just been offered an annuity at a rate of 21:1 (more later).

Even a minor difference of 1 (or £1) at this stage can have a significant effect if it is taken into account that it represents your pension income over a number of years. Some older pension schemes did provide for a protected lump sum, but this is an area I don't intend to cover here, and I would advise that you contact your financial advisor to check whether this applies to you.

Lump sum payments from small pensions

Another option which may be open to stroke survivors over the age of 60 is a small lump sum payment from their pension, where a member commutes their entire benefits from an occupational scheme in return for a one-off 'small lump sum'.

A 'small lump sum' payment may be made from a pension if the following criteria are met:

-the member must be at least 60 and not be in control of the business or the pension scheme.

-the 'small lump sum' payment is no more than £2,000 and represents the members total entitlement under the scheme.

-this is the first such payment.

The are a myriad of other conditions so I would recommend that you check with your scheme provider to see if you qualify.

Trivial commutation of pensions

Another option to consider to improve the household finances is that of trivial commutation of your pensions.

This is a useful way of gaining a benefit from any small pensions you may have. You can be given the opportunity to convert the whole (100%) of any 'small' pensions you have into one-off cash payments. This is known as 'trivial commutation' and the cash can be received as a 'trivial commutation lump sum'. As we have already seen 25% of the value of most pension schemes can be converted into tax free cash when the pension fund matures.

This is the same for trivial commutation lump sums, with 25% of the amount being free of tax and the remaining 75% being taxable.

To do this you need to be over the age of 55, qualify for access to your pension under the ill-health provisions, and have a number of pension funds valued under £30,000 in total.

As always the rules regarding this are quite complex, and I would recommend you contact your financial advisor to find out if you could benefit from this.

Summary

We will look at disability benefits for working aged people later, and we'll conclude that they really don't add up to much for working age people. Due to this the early access to pension funds is a godsend.

Furthermore, under the new state pension rules, a stroke survivor currently aged 50 will have a further 17 years before they will be eligible to claim their state pension, so access to another source of funding is essential.

Annuities and drawdown pensions.

When you come to withdraw your pension from your pension company, either before or after you have taken your 25% tax free amount, you can transfer your pension to another company who will offer you an annuity income, or continue investing it on your behalf (and will payout as and when you wish to drawdown).

Annuities

An annuity is where the pension pot (usually after the payout of the 25% tax free) is used to buy a fixed income, which will be paid for the rest of the pensioners life. The annuity received will be based on the size of the pension pot and current interest rates and health, amongst other things.

If you have built up your pension pot with, for example , the Zurich Insurance Company, and if you are unhappy with the annuity rates they are offering you, you can transfer the whole pension to, say, the Aviva Insurance Company if they are offering a higher income.

Once the annuity has been purchased the contract is usually fixed for life, which means that you will not have to think about your pension arrangements again.

It has the benefit that it secures an income for life, but the disadvantage that there will not normally be an option to renegotiate the amount at a later date.

If there are health issues which may result in a reduced life expectancy, the annuity rate can be increased, in some cases by up to 1/3rd.

Insurance companies are not as willing to gamble on life expectancy as they used to be, and the rates offered are currently low. As people are generally living longer the annuities paid are getting smaller.

The benefits offered by annuity providers can vary enormously so it is worth shopping around for the best deal. The annuity rates offered can vary, and some providers offer a number of benefits, which can include a small amount of life cover in the early years of the arrangement.

It is very easy to go online and compare the rates on offer before you tie into a contract.

Given that the whole pot is exchanged for the promised annuity it is relatively easy to calculate the payback period, and compare it with your life expectancy, to calculate whether you are getting a good deal.

The table below shows the annuity rates currently being offered. As you can see they vary with age, and some offer a guarantee of the amount, and an escalation to cope with inflationary factors.

The first table is based on an investment of £100,000, on a single life (with no benefit for the spouse after the death of the pensioner), based on a central London postcode. Slightly higher rates can be obtained in other areas of the country.

Instead of paying you a guaranteed income for the rest of your life, a fixed 'term' annuity pays you a guaranteed income only for a fixed period of time. This is helpful if you want to keep your options open, and not commit to something you cannot change later.

A fixed term annuity works by paying you an income for a set period – typically five or ten years.

At the end of this period, it then pays you a reduced lump sum of money (which will be the amount you originally invested, less the amounts you have taken as an annuity, less, of course, their fees). You can then use this to invest in another retirement income product, such as a conventional or enhanced annuity, or take as a cash lump sum, subject to tax.

Age	Level rate No guarantee	Level rate With 10 yr Guarantee	3% Escalation No guarantee
55	£4,427	£4,400	£2,667
60	£4,911	£4,866	£3,805
65	£5,563	£5,478	£3,890
70	£6,304	£6,131	£4,559
75	£7,320	£6,977	£5,632

The second table below is based on a similar investment, for a pensioner and spouse, where a percentage of the annuity continues to be paid to the spouse upon the death of the pensioner.

Age	Level rate 50% joint Life	Level rate 100% joint Life	3% escalation 50% joint Life
55	£4,106	£3,894	£2,436
60	£4,555	£4,320	£2,849
65	£5,137	£4,782	£3,376
70	£5,780	£5,337	£4,105
75	£6,733	£6,132	£5,102

As the annuity market has evolved the number of different annuity options has increased, and now there are a large number of different options for those considering an annuity income in their retirement, they are:

1. A level income annuity is one which will stay the same, and won't increase. The effect of inflation means that this income will reduce in real terms over time.
2. An increasing income annuity usually starts out as a lower amount, but will increase by a fixed amount each year.
3. An income tracking annuity, which can be set up to increase in line with the Retail Price Index (RPI). As a result of this the pension will retain its buying power by tracking inflation.
4. A single life annuity, which will pay an income for the pensioners life, but will stop upon his death.
5. A joint life annuity, with which you can select the amount of annuity income that would be paid to a beneficiary upon your death. It is possible under this arrangement for any agreed percentage of the annuity to continue to be paid, with higher amounts having the effect of reducing the income.
6. A guaranteed period annuity, where the income is paid for the pensioners lifetime, and is also guaranteed to be paid for a minimum length of time. If the pensioner dies within this time, the income will be paid to his estate or beneficiaries for the rest of the guaranteed period.

Guarantee periods of up to 30 years are available. The longer the guarantee period chosen, the less income initially received.

7. A value protection annuity, which at the end of an agreed period, will return the original investment, less any income paid over the period, to your beneficiaries.

   The initial annual income will be lower with this option. But all the money you used to buy the annuity will be repaid.

8. Impaired health annuities are offered to those suffering from a range of different medical conditions, with the annuity provider gambling on the pensioner dying sooner rather than later.

9. Smoker and enhanced annuities are offered on a similar basis, where the pensioners lifestyle is considered to lead to an earlier death.

Given the myriad of options available there are often a number of different annuity incomes offered to pensioners when they apply for an annuity. As a result of this it is difficult to compare them to assess the best option.

But, as can be seen, with all of the options available everybody's circumstances are likely to be covered. But deciding which option is for you is only half of the battle, the big decision to take is when to apply for the annuity, as the values offered can vary significantly over time.

This can be seen in the graph below, which charts, over time, the annuities offered to a 65 year old with a £100,000 pension fund, on a single life, level option, with no guaranteed period.

The current annuity offered on this basis was £5,563 pa in September 2018, and was as high as £7,908 in September 2008, and was as low as £4,696 in August 2016. Once you lock into an annuity agreement you cannot change the rate, even if the market rates have improved. You can, however, invest further amounts into the

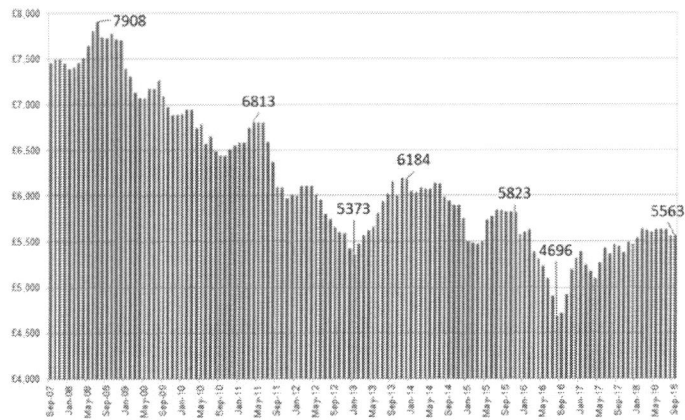

Annuity rates chart for £100,000 fund, aged 65, level and single life

agreement to increase your income.

Other than this, annuities tend to be fairly inflexible once the annuity rate has been agreed and purchased.

Annuity rates reached an all time low in August 2016 after the Brexit vote and appear likely to remain low while interest rates remain low and uncertainty continues over the trade agreement terms with the EU and other countries.

Personally, I have delayed taking out an annuity until the market picks up, but in the interim have invested in US tech stocks, which have benefitted from a rejuvenated US economy, and a strong dollar.

In the long term I am hoping for an improvement in U.K. annuity rates, but the uncertainty over Brexit and global markets, seem to make this a more long term goal.

You should note that, other than for value protected annuities, once that you buy an annuity your pension pot has gone, and should you die a short time thereafter there will be nothing left for your family.

Some pension contracts specify that an annuity has to be purchased by the age of 75.

Drawdown

Income drawdown allows you to take income from your pension fund while the fund remains invested and continues to benefit from any investment growth.

You often need a fairly substantial fund to take income drawdown although the amount of fund varies according to the pension provider.

But basically, with income drawdown you keep your funds invested and draw an income directly from it for as long as funds last.

Income drawdown provides an alternative to an annuity if you prefer to have greater control over how you receive your pension income.

There are a number of rules and restrictions regarding drawdown, and these vary from company to company.

If you opt for drawdown you can have unrestricted access to your pension pot, which gives you the financial flexibility to deal with all that life throws at you.

The main advantage that drawdown has over annuities is that you always have access to your pension pot, and upon death, that pot is still available for your family to inherit.

With drawdown giving pensioners access to their pension pot they can often land themselves in financial difficulty, by making poor decisions when withdrawing their funds. So it is often best left to the financially savvy.

The access to pension funds under the ill-health provisions allow for a retirement income, through either an annuity or drawdown, for the years prior to the receipt of the state pension.

That access can also help to provide for an additional income to supplement the state pension once it is received.

The state pension.

Provided that you have paid sufficient national insurance throughout your working life you will receive a state pension, of a maximum of £164.35 per week, when you reach the state pension age (which is currently in the process of change – more later).

You need at least 10 qualifying years, not necessarily in a row, on your national insurance record to get any State Pension.

You need at least 35 qualifying years to get the maximum pension of £164.35.

You'll get a proportion of the state pension if you have between 10 and 35 qualifying years.

You are credited with a qualifying year for national insurance if:

-you were working and paid the minimum national insurance contributions in that year.

-you were getting national insurance credits for example if you were unemployed, ill or a parent or carer (and claiming benefits) in that year.

-you were paying voluntary national insurance contributions in that year.

You do not have to stop working when you reach state pension age but you'll cease paying national insurance.

The amount of pension you'll receive depends on your cumulative national insurance record, and you can go on-line at www.Gov.UK to check your record and review the estimate of what your state pension will be .

If your starting amount is less than the £164.35, above, this may be due to you not having sufficient qualifying years.

You can get more state pension by adding more qualifying years to your national insurance record. To do this you can go online and pay the shortfall for the years indicated.

You can do this up until you reach the State Pension age.

The state pension scheme changed from 5th April 2016, and every qualifying year added after that date will add about £4.70 a week to your state pension.

This has been calculated as follows:-

£164.35/35years = approximately £4.70.

I have reviewed my own pension forecast and find that I can gain another two qualifying years if I pay two amounts of £733.20, which will prove a very good investment as long as I survive for 156 weeks past my state pension age.

Paying extra for qualifying years prior to 2016 will increase the pension by less than £4.70. You need to contact the national insurance office direct to find out how much you will gain.

The state pension increases each year by whichever is the highest:

-earnings – the average percentage growth in wages in the U.K.

-prices – the percentage growth in prices in the UK as measured by the Consumer Prices Index.

- 2.5%

The state pension is not means tested, which means that you can still receive it if you have any other income from an employment or a pension.

The state pension is paid every four weeks in arrears, with the first payment being made within 5 weeks of you reaching state pension age.

You can defer the state pension if you do not need the income when you reach state pension age. The benefit to this is that the amount you ultimately receive will be higher.

The additional pension you can receive by doing this is calculated at 1% for every 9 week's deferred (or 5.8% per year).

If you are not achieving that rate on your savings you may be better off drawing down your savings and deferring your state pension.

You can get a one-off lump sum (plus interest) if you defer your pension for at least 12 months.

If your partner is over state pension age they can inherit your deferred pension or lump sum upon your death.

With the significant changes in the state pension scheme in April 2016, and the changes to the provisions for protected payments and contracted out pensions, I would strongly advise that you take advice from your financial adviser or the Citizens Advice before you take any action regarding your state pension.

Increase in the state pension age

A lot of people think that they can rely on the State pension to fund their retirement, but even with a complete national insurance record you can only expect to receive £8,546.20 a year when you retire. You are likely to need far more for a comfortable old age.

Not only is the State pension inadequate to provide for a comfortable retirement at the moment, but the plans in place to increase the retirement date have reduced its effectiveness further.

I have included copies of the governments tables showing the effect of these changes, below.

Between October 2018 and October 2020, both men and women's state pension age will increase to 66, and between 2026 and 2028 it will rise again to 67

The changes are aimed at bringing women's state pension age into line with men's, and taking into account that everyone is living longer. There are also plans to

Table 3: Increase in State Pension age from 65 to 66, men and women

Date of birth	Date State Pension age reached
6 December 1953 – 5 January 1954	6 March 2019
6 January 1954 – 5 February 1954	6 May 2019
6 February 1954 – 5 March 1954	6 July 2019
6 March 1954 – 5 April 1954	6 September 2019
6 April 1954 – 5 May 1954	6 November 2019
6 May 1954 – 5 June 1954	6 January 2020
6 June 1954 – 5 July 1954	6 March 2020
6 July 1954 – 5 August 1954	6 May 2020
6 August 1954 – 5 September 1954	6 July 2020
6 September 1954 – 5 October 1954	6 September 2020
6 October 1954 – 5 April 1960	66th birthday

increase the retirement age to 68, as can be seen in the final table below.

Table 4: Increase in State Pension age from 66 to 67, men and women

Date of birth	Date State Pension age reached
6 April 1960 – 5 May 1960	66 years and 1 month
6 May 1960 – 5 June 1960	66 years and 2 months
6 June 1960 – 5 July 1960	66 years and 3 months
6 July 1960 – 5 August 1960	66 years and 4 months (1)
6 August 1960 – 5 September 1960	66 years and 5 months
6 September 1960 – 5 October 1960	66 years and 6 months
6 October 1960 – 5 November 1960	66 years and 7 months
6 November 1960 – 5 December 1960	66 years and 8 months
6 December 1960 – 5 January 1961	66 years and 9 months (2)
6 January 1961 – 5 February 1961	66 years and 10 months (3)
6 February 1961 – 5 March 1961	66 years and 11 months
6 March 1961 – 5 April 1977*	67

Table 5: Increase in State Pension age from 67 to 68, men and women

Date of birth	Date State Pension age reached
6 April 1977 – 5 May 1977	6 May 2044
6 May 1977 – 5 June 1977	6 July 2044
6 June 1977 – 5 July 1977	6 September 2044
6 July 1977 – 5 August 1977	6 November 2044
6 August 1977 – 5 September 1977	6 January 2045
6 September 1977 – 5 October 1977	6 March 2045
6 October 1977 – 5 November 1977	6 May 2045
6 November 1977 – 5 December 1977	6 July 2045
6 December 1977 – 5 January 1978	6 September 2045
6 January 1978 – 5 February 1978	6 November 2045
6 February 1978 – 5 March 1978	6 January 2046
6 March 1978 – 5 April 1978	6 March 2046
6 April 1978 onwards	68th birthday

Equity release- releasing some of the equity in your property.

Given the increase in house prices and with mortgages being paid off most people tend to build up a value in their homes. Often this capital cannot be accessed until the property is sold, with that amount then being received in cash.

But there are a number of options now available to homeowners to get their hands on that cash earlier.

The equity can be released from your home with either a lifetime mortgage or a home reversion scheme.

I will run through the differences between these two options below:

-A lifetime mortgage (including the drawdown lifetime mortgage option (below)) is an equity release scheme which lets the homeowner (aged from 55 to 95) release the cash tied up in their home.

It's basically a loan secured against your home that's only usually repaid when the borrower dies or goes into long-term care.

Then, the loan plus interest is repaid and the plan comes to an end.

Your house is then sold and the equity release provider will take their money from the sale proceeds. The remainder goes to your estate.

With a lifetime mortgage you retain full ownership of your home at all times.

Interest is charged on the amounts from the date that they are drawn down. You could save a lot of interest if you don't take all of the money straight away.

There are usually no payments to make as the loan, plus roll-up interest, is repaid when the plan ends, (usually upon death or when the borrower moves into long term care).

The interest accrues, meaning that it rolls up and is added to the loan. This is also known as compound interest.

Normally compound interest is something that should be avoided, as can be seen below.

A pensioner has been offered the loan of £100,000 at 10% on a simple interest or a compound interest basis, which one should he accept?

The simple interest charges 10% of the £100,000 each year, a total of £50,000, whereas the compound interest charges 10% of the accumulated balance each year, a total of £61,051.

Compound interest reflects the interest on the total borrowing as it changes each year, which means that interest is being charged on interest, with the outcome that the total debt increases by £11,051.

A lifetime mortgage is the most popular kind of equity release but there is another plan available called home reversion, which operates in an entirely different way.

-The home reversion plan. Instead of the property remaining 100% in your name, you sell all or part of your property to a reversion company in exchange for a cash lump sum representing the equity.

To do this you need to be over the age of 65, and there is no interest to pay on the money released, so there are no monthly payments to make.

As the home reversion company is not charging any interest, you need to ask whether they are solely gambling on the house price increasing, or taking their income some other way?

Home reversion plans are often priced very competitively which may result in you selling your home for less than the market value.

Once a home reversion plan has been initiated it is very difficult to reverse the process.

If you die soon after taking out the plan, you may have sold your property too cheaply.

When the plan comes to an end, the home reversion provider takes their percentage share of the sale proceeds of the house.

Even though you will no longer own all, or part of your house, you have the right to remain in your own home rent-free for the rest of your life.

Receive a tax-free cash lump sum	Lifetime Mortgage	Home Reversion
Receive a tax-free cash lump sum	Yes	Yes
Option to take more in the future	Yes	Yes
Retain ownership of your home	Yes	No
Sell a share of your home	No	Yes
No monthly payments	Yes	Yes
Interest accrues on loan	Yes	No

Value of your estate is reduced	Yes	Yes
Affect means tested benefits	Yes	Yes
Paid upon death or long term care	Yes	Yes
Benefit from increases in house prices	Yes	No

Both the lifetime mortgage and home reversion plans will reduce the value of your estate and may affect your entitlement to state benefits.

Equity release is subject to a lot of regulation, and you are prevented from taking out a lifetime mortgage or home reversion plan without verifying that you have taken independent specialist financial advice.

The amount of cash that you can release is governed by the type and value of your property, and your health and lifestyle.

The average amount released under these plans is £85,000, and is often taken either as a lump sum or a series of smaller amounts.

Generally, the older you are and the higher the value of your home, the more equity you can release.

Some plans come with a no negative equity guarantee, which means you can never owe more than the value of your home, and therefore won't risk leaving your family with a debt to repay.

There are also plans available that allow you to protect a percentage of your home's future value so that you can guarantee an inheritance. Other features include paying monthly interest and drawdown facilities, such as the drawdown lifetime mortgage.

Drawdown lifetime mortgage

A drawdown lifetime mortgage allows you more freedom to release your money when you like, and the lender agrees to an overall sum of money you can borrow, which is set aside for you.

You can take an initial lump sum and then withdraw smaller amounts when you need them.

These plans can help you to organise your finances so that you can ensure that you don't miss out on means-tested benefits.

You can benefit from any house price rise that is over and above the amount you borrowed.

As it's your home I would advise that you take specialist independent advice before considering securing a loan against it. You do have to get specialist advice before a borrower would consider lending on a equity release plan.

If you decide to go ahead with an equity release plan you should expect a fee of approximately 2% of the amount released, with a minimum of £1,500 being likely.

Moving house and downsizing to release funds.

Another way of extracting the capital you have tied up in your property is to sell it. This may fit in with your lifestyle choices, as your handicap, as a result of the stroke, may have resulted in your current home being no longer suitable for you.

If you consider the cost of installing the paraphernalia needed to make your house accessible, and the effect of that on its value, it may not make for good value for money.

Maybe that money could be better spent on professional fees on a house move, to somewhere more user friendly. Maybe a downsizing was long overdue. But there are a number of things to consider before you do.

How much is your house worth? Really, how much is your house worth? How much do you still owe on your existing mortgage?

Could you get another mortgage given your age, and the stringent rules imposed following the financial crash? Can you transfer your mortgage?

You maybe need to talk to your mortgage advisor first.

Is this the right time to sell? Is your property in good condition? Are there a lot of part-exchange opportunities available on new build developments in the area?

Get a proper valuation done, and research the best estate agents (consider the advantages and disadvantages of online versus high street agents).

Similarly, research conveyancing solicitors (again, comparing online with the high street), and take advice on which property surveys need to be undertaken.

The sale is only half the battle, the choice of a new home which is accessible for the disabled may not be so easy.

It is important that you spend longer than usual looking around a prospective purchase to ascertain whether there are any pitfalls not apparent on the first viewing.

Bear in mind that you're buying for the long term (or that this may be your home until you die).

Consider the cost of adapting the property and making it more accessible, and research the facilities available within walking distance.

With land prices being so high builders are under pressure to obtain the maximum return from their land banks. This is often resulting in the properties being built being the more expensive, 4/5 bedroom family houses.

Homes suitable for the disabled are rarely being built on the new developments, with bungalows not being as profitable to the builder as other types of property. However, developments of housing specifically for the over 50's are becoming popular. Some of these come with alarm systems linked to local medical services to help deal with medical emergencies.

These developments are often very accessible for the handicapped.

The properties are often smaller two to three bedroom bungalows, which are usually keenly priced.

The vendors of these developments are often keen to take a part-exchange property to boost their sales. But as any future sale will be restricted to the over 50's market is it a good investment?

Could the builders be persuaded to include ramps and other aids as part of the deal?

Sale of your business.

If you 're not able to return to your business and your finances dictate that you need a lump sum of cash, and none of the above opportunities fit with your personal circumstances, you may be left with the choice of selling your business.

Although this may help alleviate the immediate financial pressures, whether the amount received from the sale will be more or less than the market price of the business depends upon a number of things outside of your control.

Goodwill

The sale of your business may entail a professional valuation of the business, which will include the goodwill as well as the vehicles and equipment.

Goodwill is a premium charged when selling a business which takes into account the future earning potential of the business. Goodwill is created as the business establishes itself, and can often account for a significant amount of the sales proceeds.

It represents the amount that a buyer is prepared to pay over the value of the tangible assets, and there are details available online of goodwill valuations of different business sectors.

You need to check whether your business is in line with the industry averages.

Supply and demand

Whether you get a good price for your business may rely on the amount of similar businesses there are for sale and the number of potential buyers there are at the time you wish to sell.

If there are more businesses for sale than there are buyers, then you have a buyers market, where they can dictate the terms of the deal.

In these circumstances any potential buyers may see your eagerness to sell the business and put in a low offer for it.

If there are more buyers than businesses for sale, then you have a sellers market, where those who are prepared to pay the highest price will get the deal.

Emotional attachment

It may take many sleepless nights before you will resign yourself to the sale of your business, and you will need to get over your emotional bias.

It is likely that you have poured years of late nights and early mornings into your business. It may have been in the family for generations. You may even think of it as your part of the family.

Summary

Before this option is considered you should seek advice, as there may be tax and other implications, such as staff redundancies, to take into account.

But this option doesn't usually work as a quick fix as the average time a small business remains on the market is 6 to 8 months.

It was over three years before I managed to extricate myself from my business, mainly due to the incompetence of the professionals involved.

And are you desperate enough to possibly let your business go to ruthless buyers, with low morality and little empathy for the business, the staff and its customers.

If you decide to put your business up for sale, I would strongly advise that you contact your accountants to get your books up to date, as no-one will buy a business without details of the finances!

Potential buyers will take comfort in accounts prepared (and audited) by independent accountants.

The accountants can also advise on the Capital Gains Tax and VAT implications of the proposed sale, and may even have clients looking for a business to buy.

If the business has trusted employees it may prove quicker and cheaper to arrange for a deal where they buy the business, or take it over for the short term, in your absence.

They may prove more sympathetic in regards to the amount they pay, and will give you comfort that the business has remained in good hands.

Again, if you do decide to sell your business I would advise that you obtain specialist advice as to the state of the market, and whether the timing is right, as these can have a significant effect on the price.

If you are not ready yet to sell the business there are other options available, such as a part sale of the business, or retaining the business premises and charging a rent. Each of these options will bring its own tax costs, and specialist advice may need to be sought.

Benefits available

As a result of your stroke You may be able to claim benefits such as Employment Support Allowance or Personal Independence Payment, both of which are dependent upon an assessment of your mobility and cognitive abilities.

Employment support allowance

Employment Support Allowance (ESA) is paid if you are ill or disabled and offers you:

-financial support if you're unable to work.

-personalised assistance so that you can work if you're able to.

You can apply for ESA if you're employed, self-employed or unemployed, and you must first have a Work Capability Assessment to see to what extent your disability affects your ability to work.

Following your assessment you'll be placed in one of 2 groups if you're entitled to ESA:

-work-related activity group, where you're deemed to be fit for work.

-support group, you will usually be assigned to this group if your illness or disability severely limits what you can do.

How much ESA you get will depend upon which group you have been allocated to, and the amounts are:

-up to £73.10 a week if you're in the work-related activity group

-up to £110.75 a week if you're in the support group

To further complicate the position there are three different types of ESA, the first of which is linked to the Universal Credit claim system.

The second is the Contributory ESA which is linked to the National Insurance record of the claimant.

The third ESA is the income-related ESA, which can be paid on its own, or alongside the Contributory ESA if the income of the claimant is very low.

The amounts above vary according to your means. Your needs (and those of your partner, if you have one) are compared with the money you have, such as your income and savings.

You cannot get income-related ESA if your (and your partner's) capital or savings are over £16,000.

If you're in the support group and on income-related ESA, you may also be entitled to the enhanced disability premium at £16.40 a week.

You may also qualify for the severe disability premium at £64.30 per week.

It appears that the rules regarding this Allowance have been drafted in such a complicated manner to discourage claimants, but given that this Allowance is intended to help those in need following a stroke (or similar misfortune) I would encourage you to make a claim.

There are a large number of highly paid civil servants being paid to reject your claim for this Allowance, and it would be rude not to make a claim.

If you make a claim and get rejected don't get despondent, it is expected that you will make an appeal (see later notes).

Personal Independence payment

The Personal Independence Payment (PIP) helps meet the extra costs of long-term ill-health or disability. It is not means tested, so you can claim it while you are working.

PIP is made up of 2 parts. Whether you get one or both of these and how much you'll get depends on how severely your condition affects you. The Department of Works and Pensions (DWP) decides the severity following an assessment.

The two parts are:-

-Daily living part, which looks at the claimants ability to wash and feed, and basically look after themselves. The weekly rate for the daily living part of PIP is either £57.30 or £85.60.

-Mobility part, which looks at the claimants ability to walk unaided over a set distance. The weekly rate for the mobility part of PIP is either £22.65 or £59.75.

The assessment process has been criticised enormously, with the a large number of claimants being initially turned down, and successfully appealing against the decision of the Department of Works and Pensions.

My claim was initially turned down, and accepted upon appeal. I was astonished to find that my application, which had taken me hours to complete, and which also included medical references, had been reviewed for only 5 minutes before rejection!

I would suggest that you make a claim for PIP, with the expectation of being rejected, and then contact your local Citizens Advice for help with an appeal. It is ridiculous that the people that the benefit was intended to help are being rejected in such large numbers.

The huge care costs which the government argue are crippling the countries finances could be significantly reduced if the ESA/PIP application process was dealt with by compassionate medical professionals rather than a target driven government department.

This would reduce the excessive time and costs of the appeal procedure.

The Department for Work and Pensions (DWP) has revealed that four out of five applications were being rejected as a result of a key performance target of 80% being imposed on them.

Sir Henry Brooke, a former judge who has served as a mediator in benefit appeal cases, was cited as stating "This appears to be an absolutely outrageous interference by the executive with the rule of law."

A recent report disclosed that 18% of PIP appeals were approved at the mandatory reconsideration stage, compared to 65% of those that reach a tribunal.

I would advise that you make a claim because that's what it's there for, but don't expect a success straight away so that the refusal won't upset you.

Fortunately the appeal tribunals take into account the disabilities of the claimants, and are not governed by the government targets.

Carers allowance

If your spouse or partner will be spending at least 35 hours a week caring for you, they may be able to receive Carer's Allowance. The weekly rate is £62.70.

The recipient of the Carers Allowance also receives a National Insurance credit for state pension purposes.

In order for them to claim this you must be receiving PIP (which is another good reason to claim it!).

I would advise that you contact Citizens Advice to check whether you are entitled to claim this, and don't fall foul of any of the exclusions.

Citizens Advice

Your local Citizens Advice may be able to assist you on a number of financial matters, such as the above and the benefits calculator, which will assess which benefits (there are many) you are eligible to claim.

They can also advise you on how to deal with aggressive creditors, and making the best use of limited resources.

They can also provide explanations, and assist in claims for Jobseekers Allowance, Universal Credit and Carers Allowance.

If you get PIP you may be entitled to a number of other benefits, such as housing benefit, the carers allowance (above), a reduction in your council tax, your road tax bills and discounts on travel.

These benefits can be quite significant so should not be ignored.

You'll need your PIP award letter before you can apply for these benefits.

Housing benefit

You can get an additional amount of housing benefits if you have qualified for PIP. Housing Benefit is intended to help you with rent and some other housing costs, and you qualify for it if you pay rent, are on a low income (more later), and do not have capital in excess of £16,000.

The amount of housing benefit that you get is based on a weekly 'eligible rent', which may be less than your actual rent if restrictions apply.

As you would expect with the benefits system there are a number of restrictions that do apply, and I would advise that you ask Citizens Advice if you are considering applying for this benefit.

You can get extra amounts of Housing Benefit in the form of premiums if you meet certain disability conditions, and the Citizens Advice should be able to advise you on these.

As mentioned above you cannot get housing benefit if the household's capital is above an upper limit of £16,000.

There is also a lower limit of £6,000, and If your capital is between these lower and upper limits, it is treated as generating income.

This income has been called 'tariff income', and is calculated as follows:

£1 a week for every £250, or part thereof, above the lower limit is included as your income in the housing benefit calculation, which takes into account all the households income and needs.

For example, if you have capital of £7,000 you are deemed to have a tariff income of £4, and this income is included in the calculation to assess the benefit payable.

Given that different households will have different income and needs there is no set figure that one can use for the purposes of assessing ones eligibility for housing benefit.

With that said the benefit is intended for those on low incomes.

There are restrictions on claiming housing benefit if you are already receiving other benefits, and again I would advise that you seek the advice of the Citizen Advice services if you wish to claim this benefit.

Council Tax discounts

In addition to the above there are discounts available for the disabled (and/or their carers) when paying their council tax.

Council tax bills are generally based on the assumption that there are at least two adults living in the property.However, if only one person or no-one lives in the property (or it is treated as such) a discount can be applied to the bill.

The following are examples of people who are 'disregarded' (treated as not living in the property) when it comes to calculating council tax.

Carers providing care for at least 35 hours a week, and living in the same property as the person they care for.

This discount does not apply unless the person being cared for is over 18 and in receipt of a PIP award, and will not apply if the carer is the spouse.(separate rules apply to Scotland).

You do not have to claim Carer's Allowance to qualify for this discount, and your income and savings will not affect your eligibility. If there is more than one carer in the property, they can both be disregarded for council tax purposes as long as they all meet the conditions.

A further discount maybe available if the stroke was severe enough for the stroke survivor to qualify as a 'severely mentally impaired' person.

To be disregarded on the grounds of being 'severely mentally impaired' the person will need their GP or other medical adviser to certify that they have a permanent condition that affects their intelligence and social functioning.

They also need to be eligible for a PIP award.(note it is being eligible rather than being in receipt, but it's hard to prove one without having the other).

It means you can claim:

A 25% discount – if you live with someone with a severe mental impairment and no other adults, or only adults who have also been disregarded for council tax purposes.

A 50% discount - if you have a severe mental impairment and live alone.

A 100% discount – if you have a severe mental impairment and live with another with a similar impairment.

Other people who may be affected by stroke and may be disregarded for the purposes of council tax purposes could be long-term hospital patients or care home residents, and live-in care workers.

I did not know whether to be pleased or offended when my GP certified the shortfalls in my intelligence and social functioning.

It's always a good idea to check you're claiming all the benefits you're entitled to.

Travel savings

When you get your PIP award letter, you can also apply for benefits relating to travel, such as the disabled person's railcard which can reduce rail fares by up to 1/3rd.

The discount may also apply to the disabled person's travelling companion.

The railcard needs to be purchased and can cost up to £20 for a year, or £54 for three years.

In addition to providing cheaper train travel the card may enable the holder to obtain discounts on weekends away and discounted meals.

Another significant benefit that can be obtained as a consequence of a PIP award is a Blue Badge.

This enables holders to park on a single or double yellow lines for up to three hours, in most cases, but I would advise that you read all road notices first.

The rules for off-street parking can vary according to the property owners instructions.

You must always display the Blue Badge and the blue parking clock when you park.

The Blue Badge is not a licence to park anywhere, but is very useful to allow access to areas not available to other road users.

If you qualify for the PIP standard rate mobility component you can get a 50% reduction in vehicle tax, or 100% if you qualify for the enhanced PIP mobility rate.

If you're receiving the enhanced PIP mobility rate you are also eligible for the Motability Scheme, which can help you with leasing a car, powered wheelchair or scooter.

Your local council may also operate dial-a-ride or taxi schemes for the disabled, for example, using vouchers or tokens. You may also be eligible for a bus pass.

Claim the benefits

There shouldn't be any embarrassment about claiming benefits. The benefits system is there to support people. Benefits can provide much-needed help, and relieve the burden after stroke.

Don't think that benefits are for the long-term, as you can claim benefits for a short time while you are recovering and not able to work.

But note even if you do not need to claim benefits and/or Carers Allowance it is important that you make a claim in order to keep your national insurance record up to date for State Pension purposes.

I did not know this when I stubbornly refused to claim benefits shortly after my stroke. I would now advise that you claim the PIP award as soon as possible.

The Different Strokes leaflet 'Benefits and Financial assistance' provides a lot of detail that you may find helpful.

TIAs and seizures

TIAs or transient ischemic attacks are temporary interruptions of blood flow to the brain. They are also known as a "mini-strokes", and can often occur before the individual has experienced a major stroke.

If you suffered from an ischemic stroke it is probable that you would have experienced a TIA in the period beforehand. If you had been aware of this you could have prevented your stroke.

I include this detail now so that you are aware of the connection and can become one of my evangelists and help prevent somebody else suffer a stroke in the future.

They are otherwise known as "warning strokes" because the conditions that cause them are those which are the cause of major strokes.

In the acute phase, they look exactly the same as a stroke, and doctors now treat suspected TIA cases like strokes until proven otherwise.

TIAs typically last 2 to 30 minutes and can produce problems with vision, dizziness, weakness or trouble speaking.

They resolve on their own, usually with no permanent damage.

A mini-stroke suggests a high risk of future stroke. Even though that blockage is essentially dissolved, the TIA is a warning sign.

For the doctors that means assessing stroke risk factors, making lifestyle modifications and possibly starting medication to address issues such as high blood pressure, diabetes, or undiagnosed rhythm disturbances of the heart.

If not treated, there is a high risk of having a major stroke in the near future. People who have a TIA have a 25% greater risk of having a stroke or other serious complication within 90 days.

Up to 20% of patients with transient ischemic attacks (TIAs) progress to stroke within 90 days, half within the first 48 hours.

TIAs are often caused by the narrowing or ulceration of the carotid arteries in the neck that supply blood to the brain.

Research has shown that people who have experienced a TIA are more than 50 times more likely to experience a stroke than that expected in people of their age.

One fifth of the strokes are fatal and nearly two-thirds are disabling.

The conditions of stagnant blood flow or clotting that may cause a TIA can be found in those suffering from atrial fibrillation, large heart attacks, and severe weakness of the heart muscle (cardiomyopathy).

If you hear of anyone experiencing a TIA ensure that they seek urgent medical care, even if it means that they will consider you as an interfering nuisance.

Treatment for a transient ischemic attack is aimed at preventing a stroke, being antiplatelet therapy (blood thinners), lowering the blood pressure and the cholesterol level.

Seizures

A stroke kills off part of the brain, and can in a number of cases, leave lesions, and these lesions can be the cause of seizures. The seizures are effectively short circuits, as brain signals are interrupted around the area of the lesions.

Around 5% of people who have a stroke will have a seizure within a few weeks. The incidence of a seizure is higher for those who have experienced a severe stroke.

If you have a seizure, it does not necessarily mean that you will develop epilepsy. The risk of having a seizure lessens with time following the stroke, but a small number of people will have more than one seizure and develop epilepsy.

If you have recovered from your stroke and not experienced a seizure, your risk of developing epilepsy is low.

The seizure does not have to be a dramatic 'tonic clonic' attack that most people would associate with epilepsy, it could be something as innocuous as an absence seizure, where the sufferer goes blank, or even a tingling sensation.

Occasionally, some stroke survivors may experience chronic and recurring seizures following their stroke and a diagnosis of epilepsy may be the result.

Epilepsy is often diagnosed when there are recurrent seizures that cannot be associated with a specific cause.

A diagnosis of epilepsy means that you have a tendency to have seizures. The condition can be managed, relatively successfully, with anti-convulsant medication.

Many stroke survivors who experience seizures do not develop epilepsy, but if you have seizures a month or more after your stroke, you are more at risk of epilepsy.

If the incidence of seizures is particularly high, and the anti-convulsant medication does not appear to be working, a vague nerve stimulator (VNS) can be surgically attached to the vagus nerve in the neck.

This can work very much like a pacemaker, and control the impulses of electrical energy along the nerve, reducing the incidence of seizures.

Your neurologist is best placed to advise on the best course of treatment for you.

Carers of those suffering from seizures should be aware of the guidelines of what to do if someone is having a seizure:

If the person has fallen roll them on their side to prevent vomiting or choking

Keep the person's airway open. If necessary, grip the person's jaw gently and tilt their head back.

Cushion the person's head.

Do not restrict the person from moving unless they are in danger.

Loosen any tight clothing around the neck.

Remove any dangerous objects that the person might hit during the seizure.

Do not attempt to administer any oral medication.

Time the seizure, and note the seizure in detail in order to inform the medical services if necessary.

Stay with the person until the seizure ends, and encourage them to regain consciousness.

Once the carer and survivor get used to the seizures, and the experience becomes less traumatic, there is no need to notify the medics of every seizure.

However seizures are serious medical events and their causes need to be investigated, but if they are expected as part of an epileptic condition, and are dealt with in a calm collected manner there is no need to notify medical services every time they occur. This means that a medical team and the survivor's time are not wasted on a needless trips to hospital.

My wife and I have agreed that only if my seizures are prolonged, or if more than one occurs at a time, will we notify the emergency services. We have sufficient medication on hand so as not to require medical assistance.

If the sufferer has a seizure lasting more than 5 minutes, or more than one seizure and fails to fully regain consciousness between them, there is a danger of them experiencing a potentially fatal medical condition known as a status epilepticus. If this occurs medical assistance should be obtained immediately.

How to regain movement in the limbs.

I'm sure that this is the section that you're eager to read as the paralysis caused by a stroke can be difficult to live with, and a quick fix to regain normality is probably what you're after. Sadly, I can't give you that.

Training your brain to regain your mobility is not easy and takes time. As long as you bear this in mind you will not be disappointed.

Your journey in regaining limb movement will begin with sessions with the physiotherapists in hospital, where, initially, you will make encouraging small advances.

Don't be disheartened by the small advances, as they are signs that your mobility is on the way back.

I can remember myself being assisted in my first walking exercises in hospital by three physiotherapists, and after exhaustive effort completing only 10 metres. I can now walk unaided many miles!

Rehabilitation of physical function after a stroke usually starts as soon as you are medically stable. Going to the gym becomes a fundamental part of the survivors day in hospital.

After a few days in a hospital bed it doesn't take long for the muscles on the affected side to lose their strength, which can result in balance problems.

Efforts to move the affected limbs often cause tension elsewhere in the body, which can be painful, and very tiring.

The lack of muscle tone can have a negative affect on the joints. The shoulder, which is usually held in place by the muscles in the arm and upper torso, can pull apart under the weight of the affected arm, resulting in a subluxation, which can be very painful.

In order to remedy this condition an exercise regime is necessary to build up the muscle tone. The balance problems caused by the loss of muscle tone can also be remedied by strengthening the leg muscles.

I am a left hemiplegic stroke survivor, and it's been eight years since my stroke. I must admit that I'm not the most motivated of recoverers, but have reached the stage where I can lead, what I consider to be, a normal life. I can walk as fast, and as far as my abled-bodied friends.

However, as a proficient blues guitarist before the stroke I have to admit that my skills in that respect have not returned. I do admit that this is down to me, as I have not put in the work necessary to regain full control of my affected hand.

If I had been more motivated I know I would now be playing to a standard equal to, if not better than that before my stroke. I have found it very frustrating to undertake repetitive exercises that produce very little music.

I must admit that I have little sensation in the hand and keep dropping my plectrum, but if I decided to work more on my grip I would soon be giving Eric Clapton a run for his money.

I have mentioned the above to press home to you that your recovery is down to you, and how motivated you need to be to put in the work necessary to regain your full mobility.

Lack of funding

You may find that your physiotherapist may stop treating you when they can no longer measure any improvement in your abilities.

The lack of improvement is often called the plateau, and in my situation above, it was entirely of my own making.

The withdrawal of care may be due to the health enterprise or insurance provider that is financing the physiotherapist being very target driven with their financial support.

Unfortunately the funding available to deal with stroke survivors extends predominately to getting them mobile, and out of a hospital bed.

This partly accounts for the physiotherapists enthusiasm in the early stages of recovery, and why the assistance available tails off after discharge.

When the physiotherapists reach the conclusion that their patients have plateaued, it can affect their patients in two ways.

It can mean the end of the support and guidance from the physiotherapist, and it can further result in the patient believing that they cannot improve any further.

In the past there have been mistaken assumptions made that recovery could not improve after a certain period of time, some thought a year!

In truth recovery can take place years, or decades after the stroke, so there is no need to lose hope once your physiotherapist feels that they can no longer help you.

Foot drop. Weakness and contracture in the leg and ankle can cause 'foot drop'. This is when the foot or ankle drops down when you lift your leg to take a step.

A plastic brace known as an ankle-foot orthosis (AFO) can be used to reduce the effect of foot drop, by supporting the foot and ankle to help minimise tripping and reduce fall risks.

It is common to have to try a number of AFO's before you find one that's perfect for you, as they're often made in pre-set sizes and you need to be a pest to find one that's right for you.

Repetitive exercise

You may have already seen, in the early stages, in hospital, the repetitive frequent exercise sessions pay dividends, with many survivors regaining movement in their affected limbs.

Initially it is only fingers and toes which are re-awakened, but this can accelerate with whole limbs becoming useable again.

In order to undertake the exercises, that the physiotherapists devise, the survivor first needs to find a new connection between the brain and the affected limb. This is usually done by way of repetitive exercises.

Specifically prescribed exercises can improve the strength, coordination, balance, sensation and fitness. This is known as task-specific activity and is the most effective way to improve.

Repetition is key to improvement, so you may do movements many times.

Movement and exercises can help to reduce muscle stiffness and pain.

Tension and contortion

Admittedly, it can be very frustrating willing your limbs to move, and often survivors contort themselves in their efforts to even move even a finger.

The tension and effort involved in the exercises can add to the fatigue that so often plagues survivors.

Remember, your body did what you're asking of it, without too much effort, before the stroke, so relax. I used this as a mantra the first time I had to descend a hill.

I was sure I was going to fall over, and the posture I adopted to try to prevent this, nearly caused a fall. Don't strain and unbalance yourself.

I must admit, however, that I still tense up walking down hills, even though I tell myself it's not necessary.

Exercise and rehabilitation programs

Electrical stimulation may be used to strengthen weak muscles. Equipment such as treadmills may also be used as part of the rehabilitation program.

While you may make the most improvement in the first six months, regular activity will help you to continue your recovery.

If you have been experiencing fatigue, depression or pain since your discharge you should keep up with a regular exercise regime.

This is because exercise improves your fitness, your general health and reduces your risk of possibly having another stroke.

You could join a fitness centre or an exercise group at your local community health centre. Talk to your doctor or physiotherapist before beginning or changing an exercise program, and try to find those which cater specifically for stroke survivors.

There are specialist personal trainers and organisations which help survivors regain their mobility, such as ARNI (Action for Rehabilitation from Neurological Injury), which was set up, and is managed, by Dr Tom Balchin, a stroke survivor.

It provides specialist rehabilitation programs for survivors, and runs a training program throughout the U.K. to ensure that there are trainees available in all areas.

I recommend that you contact them at www.arni.com.uk, as I can personally vouch for the efficacy of their real-life innovative training techniques, which are completely different to expensive passive approaches which have dominated stroke rehabilitation for decades.

I have seen a grown man reduced to tears of joy at his limbs being re-awakened whilst completing one of their exercises.

ARNI are big advocates of the hand treadmill as a method of improving strength.

The exercise regimes can begin using basic equipment such as toddlers playthings, like wooden toys that can be assembled and dismantled.

Other children's toys such as Plasticine and Playdough can also prove useful in regaining dexterity in the hands.

But don't expect too much too quickly, I made the mistake of buying myself an Airfix model when I wasn't quite able to complete the assembly. I think it's still in the drawer!

Try to do a jig-saw, it's cheaper than employing a physiotherapist!

A simple thing like emptying a box of matches on the floor, and trying to pick them all back up, can provide an exercise that may help in your rehabilitation.

Whilst you're working on improving your dexterity, you should also be working on your strength.

You can do this by attaching a Theraband to the stair newel post, and pulling it at various angles to exercise different muscle groups. I would advise that you speak to your doctor before embarking on this program, as they may be able to advise on the most efficient exercises.

Interestingly, one activity which I, and others have, found most useful in recovery, is pushing a shopping trolley around a supermarket. It provides support, and the opportunity to stride out without a limp.

As you can see from the above you do not have to pay fees to attend a gym to help in your rehabilitation, as many useful exercises can be done at home.

With some imagination many of the stretching exercises that are useful to your recovery can be completed using the household furniture.

You should never stand or sit idly, you should always be trying to move a stubborn part of your body that refuses to reawaken. Force yourself to move, and use your affected side.

One exercise regime which my physiotherapist had me complete was the forced use of the affected arm. This was made possible by strapping up my good arm so I was unable to use it, meaning I had to use my affected arm for all tasks.

I found this very difficult, and must admit to cheating when my hunger got too much.

I would caution, however, that you do not undertake any course of exercise without the agreement of your medical advisors.

There are lots of exercise routines which are good for you generally, but also very useful as part of a stroke rehabilitation program, such as yoga and pilates, and I would recommend that you explore these.

Regular exercise can also have a positive effect on your mental state.

Try to encourage your carer to take part in activities with you, it will be fun.

They need to be part of the rehabilitation process, and have an input in the exercise program chosen. Their encouragement can be a good motivator.

Getting out and about is very good for improving mobility generally. Think about swimming, walking and cycling, which are all good for building up general strength, and balance.

I swim regularly in a pool, with a fixed depth of 1.3 metres, which is ideal, not only for swimming, but also for walking exercises.

Being in the pool effectively reduces my weight, making exercise easier. The initial problem I had to overcome, however, was the entry and exit from the pool, which thanks to Roman steps I did not find too difficult.

I was also lucky to find a private pool which I could hire by the hour.

Living in the countryside I find that walking is a necessity, and not an option, so I concentrated on that activity first. When I look back at videos and photographs of myself I have made amazing progress in a relatively short period of time. I'm sure you can too if you apply yourself to it.

You could also keep a video diary so that you can watch your own improvement.

When I started cycling again I bought myself a trike to compensate for my lack of balance. Once I got used to that I progressed to an electric two-wheeler, and can now transport myself about independently.

Whilst I'm mentioning cycling I would advise that you look at the Spokes fighting Strokes website, which is very inspirational.

I have been seizure free now for over a year, so could legally drive again. But as it's healthier to walk and cycle, and given the stress involved in driving, I have no compulsion to do so.

This is at odds with the goals I set myself soon after I had my stroke, when to be independently driving again was high on my list.

It's also cheaper not to own a car, and buses and trains do an adequate job transporting me.

Follow my lead and leave the car at home, I've been told it's better for the planet.

Don't expect a quick fix. While a stroke happens in an instant, recovery takes much, much longer.

Join a Facebook group of like-minded stroke survivors and exchange tips, advice, exercises and emotional support.

Use it or lose it

Don't give up on your limbs if you cannot get them to move, as there is no time limit on when a connection can be made between the brain and the muscles.

There used to be an expression 'use it or lose it' to encourage survivors to use their affected limbs, which was, erroneously linked to spasticity. Spasticity occurs when the unused muscles in a limb contract so much that the limb (including the fingers, or toes) begins to curl in.

If you find your limb beginning to curl in all is not lost, as the position is reversible through exercise.

Working with light weights, such as tin-cans from your larder, can improve muscle strength.

Summary

The key to reclaiming the movement in your limbs is simple, and is summarised below:

-aim for a goal you want to achieve.

-devise an exercise to help achieve that goal.

-break that exercise down into manageable segments.

-repeat until the goal is achieved.

I can guarantee that the above will work for you, no matter what anyone else tells you. Be careful, though, not to overtax yourself in your efforts.

If you can't find a specific goal to aim for be careful not to plateau, it's easy to accept your lack of ability and undertake most tasks in your daily life.

Problems in communication, and how to overcome them.

According to the Stroke Association 1 in 3 people will experience communication problems after having a stroke.

Whether a stroke survivor experiences communication problems following their stroke is dependent upon the severity of the stroke, and which part of the brain has been affected. As can be seen in the diagram below different areas of the brain deal

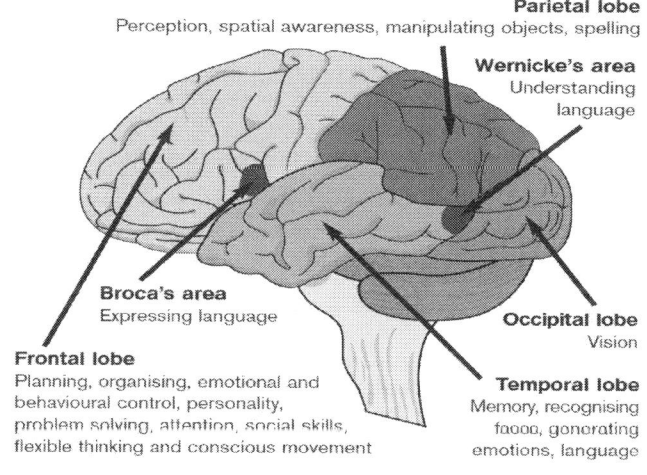

with different aspects of day to day life.

The brain is divided into two halves: the right and left hemispheres. Each hemisphere controls the opposite side of the body. If the stroke occurs on the right side of the brain, your left arm and/or leg may be weak or paralysed.

Conversely, if the stroke occurs on the left side your right arm and/or leg may be affected.

However, not all functions of the hemispheres are shared. In general, the left hemisphere controls speech, comprehension, arithmetic, and writing. The right hemisphere controls creativity, spatial ability, artistic, and musical skills.

The left hemisphere is dominant in hand use and language in most people.

In general, then, if the stroke has affected the left hemisphere the stroke survivor is more likely to have problems with the processing of language.

Following a stroke not only can the processing of language be impaired, but the paralysis or physical weakness in the face, tongue, or throat muscles can make it hard to swallow, breathe, and vocalise.

Psychological effect of the loss of communication ability on the survivor

The survivor is inherently the same person shortly after the stroke, as they were beforehand. But they are not able to express themselves in the same way.

Unfortunately people tend to associate a persons ability to communicate with their intelligence, and often tend to treat stroke survivors who are experiencing difficulties as if they are mentally retarded.

When the two statements (above) are combined with the fact that the stroke has come as an instantaneous trauma, it is not surprising that survivors can suffer greatly, but have to keep the pain to themselves.

The 'not being able to tell people what's going on' in the aftermath can extend the ordeal.

Peoples eyes don't lie when they are having difficulty understanding what they're been told by a survivor, and from a personal point of view I found it very demeaning when I was in social situations.

Carers and family can become confused and embarrassed, and question the ability of the survivor………is it the person they used to know?

For the above reasons the post - stroke rehabilitation should focus on regaining some or all of the survivors communication skills. Speech therapists specialise in communication (and their role in the recovery process is dealt with below), but nonspecialists can also play a key role.

There are three conditions that can affect communication after a stroke: aphasia, dysarthria, and dyspraxia. A stroke survivor may experience one or all of these.

Aphasia

Aphasia results from the damage to the brain. It affects the communication function but does not affect the intelligence (although it can appear that it has).

There are two different types of asphasia:

-receptive asphasia, where the survivor finds it difficult to understand long and complex sentences, especially in noisy environments. Sufferers have described the experience as trying to understand a foreign language, and find it difficult to form coherent sentences.

-expressive asphasia, where the survivor finds it very difficult to find the words, and form coherent speech, but they are able to understand other people.

Dyspraxia and dysarthria

Dyspraxia and dysarthria are related more to the physiology of speech as a result of physical damage caused by the stroke.

Survivors with dyspraxia have difficulties with co-ordination and movement of their muscles with the result that they cannot form the correct speech sounds.

Survivors with dysarthria do not suffer from finding their words but because of a physical weakness cannot form their words. They can often slur their words and sound like they are drunk.

Usually it is only their physical ability to communicate that is affected.

Often the survivor is aware of their condition, and are, in a limited way, able to make others aware also.

But there are some who are unaware that anything is wrong, as a result of their brain damage.

Because of the fatigue that many survivors suffer from they may find communicating tiring given the effort they need to put into it.

Speech therapy

Speech therapy can involve practicing forming words and is a key part of rehabilitation after a stroke.

A speech therapist can also help people who are having problems swallowing, which can often result from a stroke.

In the course of rehabilitation speech therapists may use include exercises in:

Repeating words

Following directions

Reading and writing.

And could progress to:

Conversational coaching

Using prompts to help people remember specific words

Assist with the problems in language understanding by using symbols and sign language.

The use of communication technology.

Whilst the therapist concentrates on the physiology of communication, the carer and family can work with the survivor on their conversational skills. There are a number of suggestions below which may help in this task.

Activities to encourage conversation

Singing can prove an interesting challenge as it uses a different part of the brain than that used for speaking.(there is a therapy based on singing call Melodic Intonation Therapy).

Playing cards can be fun if the survivor is encouraged to name the cards.

Reviewing old calendars and diaries may encourage conversation about old events.

Reviewing a photo album can prove useful for prompting conversations about people and events.

Discuss topical news and current affairs.

Playing games such as charades can not only be fun but can prove positive in the rehabilitation.

Build a regular time slot in your calendars to undertake the above tasks.

Do's and don't's

In order to assist with the rehabilitation it will be useful to be aware of the following do's and don't's.

Do use short sentences and stick to one topic at a time

Do ensure there is no background noise

Do reassure the person that you understand their frustration

Do write things down, if it will help.

Do look directly at the person when you are speaking to them

Do speak slowly and clearly, but use a normal tone of voice

Now here are the don't's

Don't speak too fast

Don't push them too much

Don't finish the person's sentences for them

Don't assume that they must be stupid

Don't "talk down" to the survivor.

Other tips

Encouraging the survivor to write or draw what they mean can help.

They may be able to spell words that they can't say.

Regularly practice vowel and consonant sounds.

Reciting nursery rhymes and poems.

Practice reading and writing using children's books

Medication

There have been a number of control studies where medications have been used in treating aphasia. There has not been a clear conclusion as to the efficacy of this approach and there are numerous drugs currently being used for various purposes in the rehabilitation process.

Summary

As with all aspects of stroke rehabilitation, dedication and repetition will ensure a speedy recovery.

I have not mentioned 'locked in' syndrome until this point as I have very little experience of it, but I include it here to comment that advances in technology have enabled even those in this unfortunate position to communicate.

I also mention it, so those who have not experienced that fate, can feel that even on a bad day things aren't that bad!

Restoring the family dynamic.

The stroke survivor is not the only one affected by the stroke, and they should not forget it, as the family can also be affected in a huge way.

I have covered, below, an array of the problems that families come across following a stroke, and restoring the family dynamic cannot take place without open discussion of those which the family encounter.

When a survivor has a stroke, the whole family has a stroke, as their total lifestyle gets disrupted. The active holidays with children will have to stop, not only because of mobility issues but also because of the financial constraints that the stroke has caused.

The children need to be educated that the survivor is still their parent, and that he/she needs to be treated in a different way. They may become afraid of the monstrous way that the stroke has affected their parent, but can also have fun being part of the activity rehabilitation process.

How the family is affected is dependent upon who the stroke survivor is, and the seriousness of the stroke.

If the survivor was the main breadwinner the household as a whole may suffer, and a more frugal way of life may be forced upon the family.

If the survivor was the home-maker, routines and tasks, and the responsibilities for those, may change.

If the physical handicap of the stroke is significant it may force a house move, or changes to the house to allow access.

The above may cause resentment which is often unvoiced, it is imperative that this does not happen.

The relationship of the two partners will inevitably alter as one will have suffered loss of bodily function, speech, and ultimately dignity, whilst the other will have been thrust into the role of carer.

A stroke can alter two people's lives in an instant. For the person with the stroke, simple tasks suddenly become difficult or impossible. For that person's partner, life revolves around the stroke survivor's needs, requiring many adjustments.

And while the stroke can have a negative effect on the marriage, it can also prove positive with the relationship strengthening through the partners jointly dealing with the ordeal.

The stroke may cause a reversal in roles in the relationship in terms of the partners who were previously the provider and the carer, which both parties may find difficult to accept.

The partners will have to work closely together through the rehabilitation process, and communicate on new levels to keep the relationship together.

The carer may feel a pressure to "stay strong" for the survivor, and this pressure may lead to them taking on roles that they shouldn't.

Impact on intimacy

Studies have found that sexual relationships can suffer significantly, with gender roles becoming blurred, and the survivor becoming frustrated by the loss of independence, and the constant fatigue.

The husband and wife relationship becomes a carer and patient relationship and this can have a negative effect on intimacy.

This loss in intimacy can be compounded by a number of other issues:-

The survivor may lose interest in sex, but want the relationship with their partner to be more platonic.

The survivor may lose all interest in their appearance, be it their cleanliness, clothing or cosmetics.

The survivor's anger and frustration may impact the relationship in many ways.

The fear of further stroke could prevent the survivor taking part in physical activity.

The survivors toilet needs may affect the sexual attraction between the partners.

The carer may resent the survivor for the change in their lifestyles.

Fatigue may play an increasing role in the loss of intimacy.

Muscle weakness or pain may make intimacy painful or uncomfortable.

Insecurity of the survivor being rejected.

The carer may no longer find the survivor attractive.

The survivor may not feel as desirable or attractive as they were before the stroke.

Self confidence in ability to perform may result in reticence from the survivor.

A lot of the problems may be the result of the medication prescribed to prevent further stroke.

The above problems need to be recognised and discussed between the partners before intimacy can be reclaimed.

I have deliberately included one or two comments to encourage a dialogue between the couple.

If the problems are not openly discussed the relationship can suffer significantly, and can often lead to separation.

Your health professional will have dealt with problems with intimacy before so don't feel embarrassed bringing it up.

Conversely, in rare cases some people find that their sexual desire increases, or they lose their inhibitions after a stroke. This may result in a change in their behaviour, with the result that they talk openly about sex to people they don't know.

It is vital, if the family are to successfully cope with the stroke, that honest open discussions become part of family life, and counselling undertaken if thought appropriate.

Given the problems that there may be with communication, the discussions may take place towards the end of the rehabilitation process. But note that the survivor may still be able to listen and understand in the earlier stages of recovery.

If the caring needs are significant, or the carer can't bear dealing with the pain that the survivor is suffering, some thought should be given to respite for the carer, the separation may strengthen the relationship.

It may help to formally assign the household chores, giving the survivor a sense of being of use, and being part of a team. The clarification of responsibilities is useful to prevent misunderstandings.

The impact on your social circle

The stroke will probably cause uncertainty for the survivors friends, especially upon seeing the extent of the physical damage that the stroke has caused, they may have problems dealing with the survivor.

They may start dealing with the couple in a different way, with the dominant individual being relegated.

Friendships can suffer after stroke, often because people feel awkward or stay away because they don't know how to deal with the situation.

Talk to your friends about the situation. They may not understand the impact that the stroke has had on the survivor and not realise how tired the survivor may get, and how this impacts upon their ability to get out. Be open about what the survivor needs, and what they can do to help.

The lack of income may result in a change of your social set.

Children's strokes

The detail, above, assumes that one of the adults in the household is the stroke survivor. It all changes, however, in the, less common, event of one of the children being the survivor.

Although I have no personal experience of children's strokes, I would imagine the effect on the household to be equal, if not greater, than that of an adult, and my heart goes out to those families dealing with that situation.

It's a myth that only older adults have strokes. Stroke can happen to anyone at any time, including teenagers, children, newborns, and unborn babies.

Strokes in children are more likely to occur between the 28th week of pregnancy, and 1 month after birth.

Because they occur around the time of birth they are often called perinatal strokes, and they are often as a result of the baby not getting enough oxygen while traveling through the birth canal.

Strokes in older children are usually caused by another condition that stops the flow of blood to the brain or causes bleeding in the brain.

Signs of stroke in older children are often similar to adults, but can vary widely depending on a child's age and the amount of brain damage.

Children who experience a perinatal stroke often don't show any signs of the stroke until a time after the stroke (months or years later).

This may be because they develop at a much slower pace than other children, and it is only after investigation into that, that the stroke is discovered.

Children who have more serious perinatal strokes, and experience more brain injury, might also experience seizures.

Because children's brains are still developing they can benefit more from neuroplasticity, with the result that they can make significant recoveries from strokes.

Looking after yourself……….prevent it happening again!

Getting older makes us more susceptible to having a stroke, as does having a close family member who has had one. So, other than invent a time machine or a healthier family what can be done to prevent a stroke?

You may have been aware of the following lifestyle advice for a long time, and have found it difficult to live by, but if you want to prevent another stroke you must take the advice seriously.

Exercise more

Regular exercise helps to keep weight down and lowers blood pressure, and I would advise that you exercise for 30 minutes at a moderate intensity at least five days a week.

You can achieve this target by taking a walk around your neighbourhood every day, even if you don't have a dog. You may find that you will meet many neighbours, and may start to look forward to your walk as a social experience.

Set an area of your house aside as a regular exercise place, and exercise until you are breathing hard. You do not have to exercise for 30 minutes continuously.

Look for every opportunity to exercise further, taking the stairs instead of the lift.

Experiment with Yoga or Pilates to see if you can feel any benefit from these exercise routines.

Take up an activity, such as rambling, golf or tennis (after taking advice from your doctor).

Lose weight

Carrying excess weight can bring with it a myriad of medical problems, such as high blood pressure and diabetes. It can also raise your odds of having a stroke.

If you're overweight set yourself a target to lose 10 pounds, as this can have a significant impact on your stroke risk. I would recommend that you weigh yourself frequently to prevent any unnoticeable increase in weight.

You should be aware of what your body mass index (BMI) is, and set yourself a target to stay below 25. There are many websites where you can obtain your BMI details by inputting your height and weight details.

If you have great difficulty losing weight, work with your doctor on a personalised weight loss strategy. To do this, generally, you need to limit your daily calorie input, and match it with your activity level.

As a norm, if you take in more calories than you burn off in activity you will increase in weight. But for some people it is not as simple as that, as they may metabolise different types of carbo-hydrates in different ways.

They can increase their weight even when they reduce their calorie intake. Your doctor should be able to personalise a plan that takes this into account.

Quit smoking

If you are stupid enough to be still smoking, stop it. I did, and millions of others have as well, so it's not impossible!

Smoking thickens your blood, and makes a stroke more likely. It is easier now to give up than it has ever been, with medical advice and quit-smoking aids being more available.

Most smokers don't manage to give up on their first attempt, so don't give up trying. Each attempt will bring you nearer to being a non-smoker.

If you don't give up it <u>will</u> kill you.

Lower your blood pressure

First you need to establish how high your blood pressure is, your doctor should be able to advise on this, and there are plenty of test kits available online or in pharmacies, should you want to test yourself.

High blood pressure is one of the biggest contributors to the risk of stroke in both men and women.

Monitoring it and, if it is elevated, treating it, is probably the biggest difference people can make to reduce their risk of stroke.

Your blood pressure goal should be less than 135/85, and you can achieve this by reducing the amount of salt in your diet, avoiding high cholesterol foods and eating lots of fruit and vegetables.

If you have already had a stroke you will have already been prescribed a medication to keep your blood pressure down, along with a statin to reduce your cholesterol.

Eating plenty of fish, along with grains will also prove beneficial.

Moderate your alcohol intake

Research has shown that a small amount of alcohol, say one unit, may be good for you, and actually reduce your risk of stroke.

But drinking more than two units a day can sharply increase your risk of stroke, so put the cork back in after the first glass!

The same research has shown that red wine has a chemical in it called resveratrol, which can have a beneficial effect on the brain, so if you are going to drink make sure it's a small measure of red wine.

Most bars and restaurants serve wine in the following measures:

Small.   125ml

Medium.   175ml

Large.   250ml

As the research into the effects of alcohol was undertaken in the US the healthy amounts are measured in ounces, and are as follows:

1 unit

Wine.   4 ounces (or 113ml)

Beer.   12 ounces (or 340ml) (20 ounces in a pint)

Shorts.   1.5 ounces (or 43ml)

How many years have you been drinking in excess?

Treat atrial fibrillation

Atrial fibrillation is a condition that causes the upper chambers of the heart to quiver, which prevents the heart from pumping effectively. It can result from other conditions, such as sleep apnea or thyroid disorders.

If the underlying condition can be corrected the atrial fibrillation may correct itself. The quivering, which in itself is not a major concern, can lead the sufferer feeing nauseous, weak and short of breath.

In addition to the sufferer feeling unwell the blood in their heart is more prone to clotting, and these clots can then be pumped to the brain causing a stroke.

It is estimated that up to 20 percent of stroke sufferers also have atrial fibrillation. Not only are sufferers of atrial fibrillation at a high risk of stroke, but they also have an increased risk of heart failure.

Most atrial fibrillation sufferers are prescribed blood thinners by their doctors, to prevent the formation of clots in the heart.

It is essential that those who suffer from atrial fibrillation seek treatment from a doctor, as 35 percent of those that don't, do end up having a stroke.

Atrial fibrillation sufferers also have to live a healthy lifestyle, and follow the rules above, to help prevent a stroke or heart failure.

Atrial fibrillation can weaken the heart over time, as it will be working harder to maintain the blood flow through the body.

In order to treat the condition doctors can prescribe medicines that help the heart maintain a normal rate and rhythm, in addition to prescribing blood thinners.

In some cases an electrical shock can be delivered to the heart to correct the beat, or a catheter inserted to help ablate (or destroy) the tissue that is causing the irregular beat.

Take your medication as prescribed.

Most stroke survivors will have been prescribed a number of medications following their stroke, in order to prevent a repeat event.

Normally blood pressure, diabetes, cholesterol and blood thinning medications will be prescribed.

Personally, I have been prescribed the above along with a bucket load of anti-seizure medication, and I rattle morning and evening after taking the prescribed dose.

I have recently been told that some of my medications have led to a vitamin deficiency, and been prescribed even further medications to correct the matter.

It would be a brave man (or women) who would be negligent in taking their medicines, and risk a further stroke.

Contrary to what you read in the papers these medications work, and you shouldn't risk your health on some misguided crusade.

Treat diabetes

People with diabetes are 1.5 times more likely to have a stroke than people without diabetes, this is because the excess sugar that builds up in the blood can contribute to clots in the blood supply.

This is called atherosclerosis, which is when the insulin fails to reduce the glucose in the bloodstream. Over time, this excess sugar can contribute to the buildup of clots or fat deposits inside vessels that supply blood to the neck and brain.

These clots or fat deposits can result in a narrowing of the walls of the blood vessels, and interrupt the blood flow to the brain, and cause a stroke.

It is important to monitor your blood sugar regularly, and monitors to do this can be obtained easily.

Diabetics can use diet, exercise, and medicines to keep their blood sugar within a safe range.

Summary

By following the advice above you can reduce the risk of stroke significantly, although there are other general risk factors that you can do nothing about.

The risk of having a stroke doubles with every decade of age over the age of 55.

Race also plays a significant role in stroke risk, with African-Americans having a greater risk of death from stroke than Caucasians.

Gender can also affect the risk, with women more likely to have strokes than men.

Those who have already had a stroke, heart attack, or TIA are at an increased risk of having a stroke.

Even if these general risk factors apply to you, if you lead a healthy life by following the advice above, you are less likely to suffer a stroke.

Dealing with stroke can make you stronger

When you have reached the stage where you feel you have been fully rehabilitated please read below:

"If you bear in mind what you've been through, and how you've coped with it, you must agree that you've been strong enough to survive an ordeal.

Although physically you might not think of yourself as strong, but if you think of the mental challenges that you have taken on and won, you have been strong.

There's many who would look on your appearance with pity who would not have the strength of character to deal with what you have…..be proud of yourself."

Your stroke has made you a stronger person.

Further assistance

I have included details below of organisations that can help stroke survivors and their families, and I would recommend that you contact them if you are finding your new life difficult.

Different Strokes

A registered charity providing a unique service to younger stroke survivors throughout the United Kingdom. Run by stroke survivors, for stroke survivors. Most of the staff are Stroke survivors or family members and have a close personal connection to stroke. Further details can be found at www.differentstrokes.co.uk

The Stroke Association

The Stroke Association is a charity in the United Kingdom. It works to prevent stroke, and to support everyone touched by stroke, fund research, and campaign for the rights of stroke survivors of all ages. Further details can be found at www.stroke.org.uk

Access to Work

Can help you if your health or disability affects the way you do your job, and if your condition is likely to last 12 months or more. It gives you and your employer advice and support with extra costs which may arise because of your needs at work. Further details can be found at www.gov.uk/access-to-work.

Fit for Work

Can help you plan for your return to work. It offers advice and support from occupational health specialists. You will be assigned a case manager who can also work with your employer and agencies such as Access to Work on your behalf. Further details can be found at www.fitforwork.org.

Details of the author

Paul Kendall is a retired Chartered Accountant who experienced a stroke in July 2010.

He has found that the stroke changed his life for the better, and calls it his 'stroke of luck'. He is now able to spend more time with his family, and concentrate more on the 'important things in life'.

He has worked hard in regaining a lot of his cognitive and mobility abilities, and has set up and runs the Carlisle Different Strokes group, which has trained its own exercise co-ordinator to provide specialist exercise classes for its members.

He was prompted to write this book when he realised that there was very little practical advice to help stroke survivors and their families deal with a stroke.

He noted that a lot of stroke survivors had no access to financial advice, and that most thought they could not afford it. This book covers in some detail the opportunities available to minimise the financial damage that the stroke has caused.

This is book is intended as a guide to how to live a happy life after your stay in hospital.

It is basically a handbook on how to cope with the devastation of a stroke.

Acknowledgements

I would like to thank my wife Sue for her infinite patience whilst I have been writing this, and to Google, who have been on hand to validate the details as I have been compiling the facts.

I would also like to thank Heidi and Saskia, and Thomas Tosh for the use of their respective sofas whilst I have been writing.

I would also like to thank the members of the Carlisle Different Strokes Club who have provided me with the inspiration to write this book.

In particular, I would like to thank those who assisted in reviewing my draft and assisting in the production of the final version of the book.

I reserve my final thanks for those who have shown their recognition of their faith in me. Without them I wouldn't have had the confidence to complete this mammoth task.

Copyright

Published in 2019 by Paul Kendall in England

The moral right of the author has been asserted. All rights reserved. No part of this publication may be reproduced, stored in a retrieval system, or transmitted, in any form or by any means without the prior written permission of the publisher, nor be otherwise circulated in any form of binding or cover other than that in which it is published and without a similar condition being imposed on the subsequent purchaser.

Copyright © Paul Kendall

Printed in Great Britain
by Amazon